Conquer Your Year

Conquer Your Year

The Ultimate Planner to Get More Done,
Grow Your Business,
and Achieve Your Dreams

NATALIE MACNEIL

A TarcherPerigee Book

tarcherperigee

An imprint of Penguin Random House LLC
375 Hudson Street, New York, New York 10014

Most TarcherPerigee books are available at special quantity discounts for bulk purchase for sales promotions, premiums, fund-raising, and educational needs. Special books or book excerpts also can be created to fit specific needs. For details, write: SpecialMarkets@penguinrandomhouse.com.

ISBN: 9780143130123

Printed in the United States of America

3   5   7   9   10   8   6   4   2

INTRODUCTION

You're here. And I know it's for a reason. Welcome to *Conquer Your Year*, a planning system designed specifically for ambitious entrepreneurs like you— to do more, create more, live more, and grow your business with powerful intention.

I'm so excited you're reading this because that means you're on the brink of an incredible adventure. Inside these gorgeous pages, you'll create your plan, track your progress, hold yourself accountable every step of the way, and make major moves in your business and life. This is an amazing place to be, Conqueror. Are you starting to feel that tingle of excitement running up your spine? Me too.

Conquer Your Year builds on the framework of *The Conquer Kit*, helping you break down that twelve-month business plan quarter to quarter, week to week, and day to day for the year.

This is all based on how I plan my own year, meshing creativity with strategy, fun with getting it done, passionate purpose with profit.

I believe that the goals kindled deep within our hearts are the biggest kind.

....

BIGGER THAN YOUR BOTTOM LINE.

BIGGER THAN ANY NEGATIVE RESPONSE A NAYSAYER MIGHT SEND YOU.

BIGGER THAN ANY FEAR OR DOUBT YOU'RE TRYING TO WORK THROUGH.

....

That's what *Conquer Your Year* is here to help you discover, and plan for.

Yes, it'll help you make amazing things. Yes, it'll help you plan for the growth and expansion of your business. But it's also designed to help you live your life with more intention, passion, and clarity than ever.

After all, charting a course for greatness goes beyond checklists and deadlines.

Those *are* elements, of course. But we're going further than that, to focus on things like fulfillment and balance alongside launch dates and on making progress in happiness, health, and relationships even as you build your business.

Conquer Your Year is organized into twelve-week sprints that set you up to achieve a major goal in your business and make time for personal growth too, in areas like adventure, health, giving, and learning.

After all, personal growth and business growth go hand in hand.

You may ask, "Why twelve-week sprints?" If you talk to some of the successful entrepreneurs you look up to, you'll likely find many of them work in a similar way. Switching out of "do it all, all the time" mode frees you up to fiercely focus on one major goal in your business per quarter.

So many entrepreneurs do themselves a disservice by trying to do too much at once. They want to launch a game-changing new product while working on a book, traveling to speak at events, adding thousands of new subscribers to their email list, and getting a new web presence out into the world.

Does that sound overwhelming or, dare you admit, familiar? Inevitably, the ball drops on one goal. Then another. And the whole thing comes tumbling down till we're back to square one, feeling completely discouraged.

That's what makes this approach different. With *Conquer Your Year*, you'll be sprinting to one, maybe two at the most, big-but-manageable goals every twelve weeks. That way, you get it done (and done right!) the first time. Then, you're energized, motivated, and ready for your next step.

This is how great businesses are born.

Like I said, the sprints aren't just about achieving your big business goal, but also about developing and maintaining positive momentum in every facet of your life. How many times have you gotten so enthralled in a goal you were working toward that you let your health, relationships, and overall well-being slide? Now you have a business planner that takes nourishing your mind, body, and soul into consideration.

This is the 360-degree approach to conscious creation, Conqueror. Life and work, ambition and self-care woven into the same process of growth.

Now—it's time to get going.

It's time to get more done than you ever imagined.

It's time to bring your boldest dreams into reality.

It's time to feel good about every area of your life.

And it's time to *Conquer Your Year.*

Are you with me?

Let's do this.

Natalie

....

BEFORE WE DIVE IN, GO TO CONQUERYOURYEAR.COM/BOOKBONUS TO DOWNLOAD A FREE PACKAGE OF BONUSES I CREATED FOR YOU THAT GO ALONG WITH THIS BOOK, INCLUDING A LOOK AT HOW I USE THE SPRINTS AND WEEKLY LAYOUTS FROM *CONQUER YOUR YEAR* IN MY OWN BUSINESS.

....

GETTING
STARTED

YOUR WORD OF THE YEAR

Before we dive into setting your goals for the year ahead, consider your intention for the year. I pick a new intention word, sometimes words, for each fresh year.

To give you some ideas, here are a few that have been shared with me on social media from people working through The Conquer Kit: Sovereign, Aligned, Divine, Conquer (as expected! ;)), Tuned In, Kind Strength, Connected, Alive, Powerfully Present.

Your turn. Write your word in the space below. Or, if you want to get creative and crafty, you can look through magazines and photos to find a word or intention that resonates with you. Then, cut and paste it into the space below:

YOUR BIGGER PICTURE PLAN

The thing about big goals is they can be super overwhelming.

Whether you're setting up to make your first major move or your fiftieth, it's still so easy to worry your big dreams are total pie-in-the-sky, out-of-reach fantasies.

You might wonder if you should tone it down *just a little*?

AND THE ANSWER IS, IF YOU CAN BREAK THEM DOWN INTO ACTIONABLE STEPS—NO WAY. KEEP YOUR DREAMS *BIG*.

Making big goals means you're playing full-out and striving to reach them. You're pushing yourself to discover new limits and find new avenues for your potential. And that is an amazing zone to live your life in.

But you *do* need to learn how to break your massive dreams into doable, actionable micro-goals along the way.

After all, it's easy to lose motivation and give up if you're not making instant progress, isn't it? That's why marking your path with smaller goals that add up (and give you a string of small victories to celebrate) is so important.

Not sure how to make that happen? I've got just the tool you need (and you've already got access to it!).

Before you get started using this planner, you'll be working through your Bigger Picture Plan for the twelve months ahead. (This is one of the most popular exercises from *The Conquer Kit*.)

Your Bigger Picture Plan is made up of the major goals you want to achieve for the year ahead. I usually set five Bigger Picture Goals, but go with what feels right for you. *Conquer Your Year* is structured around twelve-week sprints, thus four Bigger Picture Goals may make sense to you, so you can tackle one each sprint. Some goals overlap with each other and sometimes you have a team that can work on achieving a goal in your business without much involvement for you. In those cases, you may tackle more than five Bigger Picture Goals in a year. The choice is yours. There is no right way or wrong way here.

For each Bigger Picture goal, identify five specific milestones, with approximate due dates, to keep you on track.

Here's an example of top-level, five milestone action steps for a bigger goal.

Let's say one of your five Bigger Picture Goals is to launch a new website.

Your strategic milestones may look something like this:

1. Create a mood board on Pinterest with designs, textures, patterns, colors, and fonts to determine the overall look and feel.

2. Write (or hire a pro copywriter to help you write) copy for the home page, an opt-in offer, the about page, a products/offerings page, and the contact page.

3. Create a shot list for a photographer and book a photo shoot.

4. Share your mood board, photos, and content with a professional designer to create the website.

5. Launch the website.

These milestones get broken down further into tasks and to-dos when you set up the quarterly sprint that focuses on getting the new website done.

Once you have your Bigger Picture Goals and the milestones that go with them, you'll create a vision board for each goal. This is meant to help you visualize what your life will look like after you've achieved what you've set out to conquer. So get out those old magazines or start pinning on Pinterest, if you'd rather do it digitally, and let's start picking up some momentum, shall we?

Bigger Picture Goal 1: _____

Strategic Milestones and Actions:

1.

2.

3.

4.

5.

VISION BOARD

Bigger Picture Goal 2: _____

Strategic Milestones and Actions:

1.

2.

3.

4.

5.

VISION BOARD

Bigger Picture Goal 3: _____

Strategic Milestones and Actions:

1.

2.

3.

4.

5.

VISION BOARD

Bigger Picture Goal 4: _____

Strategic Milestones and Actions:

1.

2.

3.

4.

5.

VISION BOARD

Bigger Picture Goal 5:

Strategic Milestones and Actions:

1.

2.

3.

4.

5.

VISION BOARD

Once you have your Bigger Picture Plan, let it be a compass for you throughout the year. When any new opportunity or request drops into your orbit, consider whether it is in alignment with what you truly want before saying yes.

Having clear-cut milestones allows you to prioritize, focus, and get stuff done in record time—it prevents you from filling up your schedule with all the things you agreed to do because you feel obligated rather than aligned. Give yourself permission to say no to the things that just don't fit within your Bigger Picture Plan.

THE TWELVE-WEEK SPRINTS

When you're done with your Bigger Picture Plan, you'll be ready to plan your first twelve-week sprint.

At the start of each sprint (there will be four for the year), you'll find a page dedicated to planning the broader scope of your goals.

In this section you'll plan the following:

- Your Bigger Picture milestones (the ones you set in your Bigger Picture Plan).

- Your "brain dump," which includes every task you can think of for each milestone you've listed.

- Other smaller goals for developing new habits, playing and adventuring more, giving back, taking care of your health and relationships, and so on.

- Details about content you want to create over the twelve weeks and when you'll be looking to create and publish them.

- And, of course, a reward for yourself! (Whether it's a spa day, a vacation, a book you've been dying to buy, or beyond.) You're making big moves, Conqueror. Why wouldn't you have a trophy waiting for you at the end of the race?

THE WEEKLY LAYOUT

Once your twelve weeks are mapped we move on to the week-by-week planning phase.

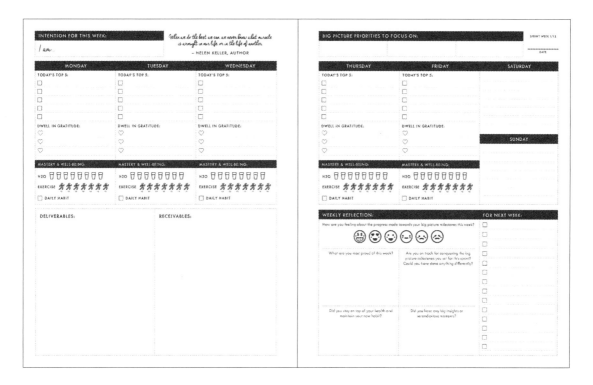

This is your nitty-gritty planning phase. You'll outline tasks for each week of your twelve-week journey so you can make powerful, steady progress with total clarity. Plus, when you're so busy from moving so quickly, having your days planned ahead of time is key.

Beyond just to-dos and checklists and deadlines, you'll also be sharing soul-centered things too, like:

- What you're grateful for.

- Your top five things to get done each day. These aren't any to-do items or errands. These are the tasks that will propel you forward toward your goals.

- How much water you're drinking and how much exercise you're getting. Color in a water doodle for each glass of water you drink. Have you read the research on the connections between hydration and productivity, and movement and creativity? Important stuff! Color in an exercise doodle for every fifteen minutes of exercise. These exercise blocks definitely don't have to be completed at a gym. This could be a fifteen minute walk, or a block of time to stretch part way through the day. It's about getting up from your desk and moving your body.

- Reflections on the week when it's over.

- What you're most proud of.

- Any insights you've picked up along the way.

Every week you'll fill in the blanks to track the progress you've made and get an idea of what's to come—so you can remind yourself how far you are already. See? I told you this planner was awesome.

You're about to infuse your life with mindful intention and deep awareness like never before. You're about to embark on the greatest adventure of all: your life. With a clear head and a full heart.

On your mark, get set . . .

Go!
Here is your
first sprint
of the year!

Sprint: _____

You are worthy of every wish, dream, goal, and desire in your heart for the year ahead.

BIG PICTURE MILESTONES

1
2
3
4
5
6
7

BRAIN DUMP

List every task you can think of for each milestone above.

☐ **PUT THESE INTO A PROJECT MANAGEMENT SYSTEM AND ASSIGN DEADLINES**

I believe that personal growth and business go hand in hand. If you want success on the outside, you have to do the work on the inside.

- NATALIE MACNEIL

BALANCED AMBITION

HABIT:	LEARNING:	GIVING BACK:

HEALTH:	RELATIONSHIPS:	ADVENTURE:

CONSCIOUS CREATION

What are you creating to share your talents and gifts with the world?

BLOG POST, VIDEO OR SOCIAL MEDIA CONTENT I WANT TO CREATE	OUTLINE	DRAFT	EDIT	PUBLISH

VISUALIZATION

What will your life look like and feel like if you conquer these goals and milestones?

SPRINT REWARD

How will you reward yourself for achieving these milestones and goals?

I am...

Striving for excellence motivates you; striving for perfection is demoralizing.

— HARRIET BRAIKER, AUTHOR

MONDAY	TUESDAY	WEDNESDAY

TODAY'S TOP 5:

☐

☐

☐

☐

☐

DWELL IN GRATITUDE:

♡

♡

♡

TODAY'S TOP 5:

☐

☐

☐

☐

☐

DWELL IN GRATITUDE:

♡

♡

♡

TODAY'S TOP 5:

☐

☐

☐

☐

☐

DWELL IN GRATITUDE:

♡

♡

♡

MASTERY & WELL-BEING:

H2O 🥛🥛🥛🥛🥛🥛🥛

EXERCISE 🏃🏃🏃🏃🏃🏃🏃
15 15 15 15 15 15 15

☐ DAILY HABIT

MASTERY & WELL-BEING:

H2O 🥛🥛🥛🥛🥛🥛🥛

EXERCISE 🏃🏃🏃🏃🏃🏃🏃
15 15 15 15 15 15 15

☐ DAILY HABIT

MASTERY & WELL-BEING:

H2O 🥛🥛🥛🥛🥛🥛🥛

EXERCISE 🏃🏃🏃🏃🏃🏃🏃
15 15 15 15 15 15 15

☐ DAILY HABIT

DELIVERABLES:

RECEIVABLES:

BIG PICTURE PRIORITIES TO FOCUS ON:

DATE

THURSDAY

TODAY'S TOP 5:

☐
☐
☐
☐
☐

DWELL IN GRATITUDE:

♡
♡
♡

MASTERY & WELL-BEING:

H2O 🥛🥛🥛🥛🥛🥛

EXERCISE 🏃🏃🏃🏃🏃🏃
15 15 15 15 15 15

☐ DAILY HABIT

FRIDAY

TODAY'S TOP 5:

☐
☐
☐
☐
☐

DWELL IN GRATITUDE:

♡
♡
♡

MASTERY & WELL-BEING:

H2O 🥛🥛🥛🥛🥛🥛

EXERCISE 🏃🏃🏃🏃🏃🏃
15 15 15 15 15 15

☐ DAILY HABIT

SATURDAY

SUNDAY

WEEKLY REFLECTION:

How are you feeling about the progress made towards your big picture milestones this week?

😁 😍 😊 😐 😕 😞

What are you most proud of this week?

Are you on track for conquering the big picture milestones you set for this sprint? Could you have done anything differently?

Did you stay on top of your health and maintain your new habit?

Did you have any big insights or serendipitous moments?

FOR NEXT WEEK:

☐
☐
☐
☐
☐
☐
☐
☐
☐
☐
☐
☐
☐
☐

The ultimate inspiration is the deadline.

– NOLAN BUSHNELL, FOUNDER OF ATARI, INC.

MONDAY	TUESDAY	WEDNESDAY
TODAY'S TOP 5:	**TODAY'S TOP 5:**	**TODAY'S TOP 5:**
☐	☐	☐
☐	☐	☐
☐	☐	☐
☐	☐	☐
☐	☐	☐
DWELL IN GRATITUDE:	**DWELL IN GRATITUDE:**	**DWELL IN GRATITUDE:**
♡	♡	♡
♡	♡	♡
♡	♡	♡

MASTERY & WELL-BEING:	MASTERY & WELL-BEING:	MASTERY & WELL-BEING:
H2O ⬚⬚⬚⬚⬚⬚⬚⬚	H2O ⬚⬚⬚⬚⬚⬚⬚⬚	H2O ⬚⬚⬚⬚⬚⬚⬚⬚
EXERCISE 🏃🏃🏃🏃🏃🏃🏃	EXERCISE 🏃🏃🏃🏃🏃🏃🏃	EXERCISE 🏃🏃🏃🏃🏃🏃🏃
15 15 15 15 15 15 15	15 15 15 15 15 15 15	15 15 15 15 15 15 15
☐ DAILY HABIT	☐ DAILY HABIT	☐ DAILY HABIT

DELIVERABLES:

RECEIVABLES:

THURSDAY

TODAY'S TOP 5:

☐
☐
☐
☐
☐

DWELL IN GRATITUDE:

♡
♡
♡

MASTERY & WELL-BEING:

H2O ⬜⬜⬜⬜⬜⬜⬜

EXERCISE 🚶🚶🚶🚶🚶🚶🚶
       15 15 15 15 15 15 15

☐ DAILY HABIT

FRIDAY

TODAY'S TOP 5:

☐
☐
☐
☐
☐

DWELL IN GRATITUDE:

♡
♡
♡

MASTERY & WELL-BEING:

H2O ⬜⬜⬜⬜⬜⬜⬜

EXERCISE 🚶🚶🚶🚶🚶🚶🚶
       15 15 15 15 15 15 15

☐ DAILY HABIT

SATURDAY

SUNDAY

WEEKLY REFLECTION:

How are you feeling about the progress made towards your big picture milestones this week?

What are you most proud of this week?

Are you on track for conquering the big picture milestones you set for this sprint? Could you have done anything differently?

Did you stay on top of your health and maintain your new habit?

Did you have any big insights or serendipitous moments?

FOR NEXT WEEK:

☐
☐
☐
☐
☐
☐
☐
☐
☐
☐
☐
☐
☐
☐

I am...

I want you to be everything that's you, deep at the center of your being.

– CONFUCIUS, CHINESE PHILOSOPHER

MONDAY	TUESDAY	WEDNESDAY
TODAY'S TOP 5:	TODAY'S TOP 5:	TODAY'S TOP 5:
☐	☐	☐
☐	☐	☐
☐	☐	☐
☐	☐	☐
☐	☐	☐
DWELL IN GRATITUDE:	DWELL IN GRATITUDE:	DWELL IN GRATITUDE:
♡	♡	♡
♡	♡	♡
♡	♡	♡
MASTERY & WELL-BEING:	MASTERY & WELL-BEING:	MASTERY & WELL-BEING:
H2O 🥛🥛🥛🥛🥛🥛🥛🥛	H2O 🥛🥛🥛🥛🥛🥛🥛🥛	H2O 🥛🥛🥛🥛🥛🥛🥛🥛
EXERCISE 15 15 15 15 15 15 15	EXERCISE 15 15 15 15 15 15 15	EXERCISE 15 15 15 15 15 15 15
☐ DAILY HABIT	☐ DAILY HABIT	☐ DAILY HABIT

DELIVERABLES:

RECEIVABLES:

THURSDAY

TODAY'S TOP 5:

- ☐
- ☐
- ☐
- ☐
- ☐

DWELL IN GRATITUDE:

- ♡
- ♡
- ♡

MASTERY & WELL-BEING:

H2O ▯ ▯ ▯ ▯ ▯ ▯ ▯

EXERCISE 🏃 🏃 🏃 🏃 🏃 🏃 🏃
15 15 15 15 15 15 15

☐ DAILY HABIT

FRIDAY

TODAY'S TOP 5:

- ☐
- ☐
- ☐
- ☐
- ☐

DWELL IN GRATITUDE:

- ♡
- ♡
- ♡

MASTERY & WELL-BEING:

H2O ▯ ▯ ▯ ▯ ▯ ▯ ▯

EXERCISE 🏃 🏃 🏃 🏃 🏃 🏃 🏃
15 15 15 15 15 15 15

☐ DAILY HABIT

SATURDAY

SUNDAY

WEEKLY REFLECTION:

How are you feeling about the progress made towards your big picture milestones this week?

😁 😍 🙂 😐 😟 😩

What are you most proud of this week?

Are you on track for conquering the big picture milestones you set for this sprint? Could you have done anything differently?

Did you stay on top of your health and maintain your new habit?

Did you have any big insights or serendipitous moments?

FOR NEXT WEEK:

- ☐
- ☐
- ☐
- ☐
- ☐
- ☐
- ☐
- ☐
- ☐
- ☐
- ☐
- ☐
- ☐
- ☐

I am...

MONDAY	TUESDAY	WEDNESDAY

TODAY'S TOP 5:

☐

☐

☐

☐

☐

DWELL IN GRATITUDE:

♡

♡

♡

TODAY'S TOP 5:

☐

☐

☐

☐

☐

DWELL IN GRATITUDE:

♡

♡

♡

TODAY'S TOP 5:

☐

☐

☐

☐

☐

DWELL IN GRATITUDE:

♡

♡

♡

MASTERY & WELL-BEING:

H2O ⬚ ⬚ ⬚ ⬚ ⬚ ⬚ ⬚ ⬚

EXERCISE 🏃 🏃 🏃 🏃 🏃 🏃 🏃
15 15 15 15 15 15 15

☐ DAILY HABIT

MASTERY & WELL-BEING:

H2O ⬚ ⬚ ⬚ ⬚ ⬚ ⬚ ⬚ ⬚

EXERCISE 🏃 🏃 🏃 🏃 🏃 🏃 🏃
15 15 15 15 15 15 15

☐ DAILY HABIT

MASTERY & WELL-BEING:

H2O ⬚ ⬚ ⬚ ⬚ ⬚ ⬚ ⬚ ⬚

EXERCISE 🏃 🏃 🏃 🏃 🏃 🏃 🏃
15 15 15 15 15 15 15

☐ DAILY HABIT

DELIVERABLES:

RECEIVABLES:

THURSDAY

TODAY'S TOP 5:

- [ ]
- [ ]
- [ ]
- [ ]
- [ ]

DWELL IN GRATITUDE:

♡
♡
♡

MASTERY & WELL-BEING:

H2O 🥛🥛🥛🥛🥛🥛🥛

EXERCISE 🏃15 🏃15 🏃15 🏃15 🏃15 🏃15 🏃15

- [ ] DAILY HABIT

FRIDAY

TODAY'S TOP 5:

- [ ]
- [ ]
- [ ]
- [ ]
- [ ]

DWELL IN GRATITUDE:

♡
♡
♡

MASTERY & WELL-BEING:

H2O 🥛🥛🥛🥛🥛🥛🥛

EXERCISE 🏃15 🏃15 🏃15 🏃15 🏃15 🏃15 🏃15

- [ ] DAILY HABIT

SATURDAY

SUNDAY

WEEKLY REFLECTION:

How are you feeling about the progress made towards your big picture milestones this week?

What are you most proud of this week?

Are you on track for conquering the big picture milestones you set for this sprint? Could you have done anything differently?

Did you stay on top of your health and maintain your new habit?

Did you have any big insights or serendipitous moments?

FOR NEXT WEEK:

- [ ]
- [ ]
- [ ]
- [ ]
- [ ]
- [ ]
- [ ]
- [ ]
- [ ]
- [ ]
- [ ]
- [ ]
- [ ]
- [ ]

I am...

*Make sure you visualize what you really want,
not what someone else wants for you.*

— JERRY GILLIES, AUTHOR

MONDAY	TUESDAY	WEDNESDAY

MONDAY

TODAY'S TOP 5:
- ☐
- ☐
- ☐
- ☐
- ☐

DWELL IN GRATITUDE:
- ♡
- ♡
- ♡

MASTERY & WELL-BEING:

H2O ⬜⬜⬜⬜⬜⬜⬜⬜

EXERCISE 🏃🏃🏃🏃🏃🏃🏃
15 15 15 15 15 15 15

☐ DAILY HABIT

TUESDAY

TODAY'S TOP 5:
- ☐
- ☐
- ☐
- ☐
- ☐

DWELL IN GRATITUDE:
- ♡
- ♡
- ♡

MASTERY & WELL-BEING:

H2O ⬜⬜⬜⬜⬜⬜⬜⬜

EXERCISE 🏃🏃🏃🏃🏃🏃🏃
15 15 15 15 15 15 15

☐ DAILY HABIT

WEDNESDAY

TODAY'S TOP 5:
- ☐
- ☐
- ☐ '
- ☐
- ☐

DWELL IN GRATITUDE:
- ♡
- ♡
- ♡

MASTERY & WELL-BEING:

H2O ⬜⬜⬜⬜⬜⬜⬜⬜

EXERCISE 🏃🏃🏃🏃🏃🏃🏃
15 15 15 15 15 15 15

☐ DAILY HABIT

DELIVERABLES:

RECEIVABLES:

BIG PICTURE PRIORITIES TO FOCUS ON:

DATE

THURSDAY

TODAY'S TOP 5:

- [ ]
- [ ]
- [ ]
- [ ]
- [ ]

DWELL IN GRATITUDE:

♡
♡
♡

MASTERY & WELL-BEING:

H2O 🥛🥛🥛🥛🥛🥛🥛🥛

EXERCISE 🏃🏃🏃🏃🏃🏃🏃
15 15 15 15 15 15 15

- [ ] DAILY HABIT

FRIDAY

TODAY'S TOP 5:

- [ ]
- [ ]
- [ ]
- [ ]
- [ ]

DWELL IN GRATITUDE:

♡
♡
♡

MASTERY & WELL-BEING:

H2O 🥛🥛🥛🥛🥛🥛🥛🥛

EXERCISE 🏃🏃🏃🏃🏃🏃🏃
15 15 15 15 15 15 15

- [ ] DAILY HABIT

SATURDAY

SUNDAY

WEEKLY REFLECTION:

How are you feeling about the progress made towards your big picture milestones this week?

😁 😍 😊 😐 😕 😞

What are you most proud of this week?

Are you on track for conquering the big picture milestones you set for this sprint? Could you have done anything differently?

Did you stay on top of your health and maintain your new habit?

Did you have any big insights or serendipitous moments?

FOR NEXT WEEK:

- [ ]
- [ ]
- [ ]
- [ ]
- [ ]
- [ ]
- [ ]
- [ ]
- [ ]
- [ ]
- [ ]
- [ ]
- [ ]

INTENTION FOR THIS WEEK:

I am...

MONDAY	TUESDAY	WEDNESDAY
TODAY'S TOP 5:	**TODAY'S TOP 5:**	**TODAY'S TOP 5:**
☐	☐	☐
☐	☐	☐
☐	☐	☐
☐	☐	☐
☐	☐	☐
DWELL IN GRATITUDE:	**DWELL IN GRATITUDE:**	**DWELL IN GRATITUDE:**
♡	♡	♡
♡	♡	♡
♡	♡	♡

MASTERY & WELL-BEING:	MASTERY & WELL-BEING:	MASTERY & WELL-BEING:
H2O ⬜⬜⬜⬜⬜⬜⬜⬜	H2O ⬜⬜⬜⬜⬜⬜⬜⬜	H2O ⬜⬜⬜⬜⬜⬜⬜⬜
EXERCISE 🏃🏃🏃🏃🏃🏃🏃 (15 each)	EXERCISE 🏃🏃🏃🏃🏃🏃🏃 (15 each)	EXERCISE 🏃🏃🏃🏃🏃🏃🏃 (15 each)
☐ DAILY HABIT	☐ DAILY HABIT	☐ DAILY HABIT

DELIVERABLES:

RECEIVABLES:

BIG PICTURE PRIORITIES TO FOCUS ON:

DATE

THURSDAY	FRIDAY	SATURDAY

THURSDAY

TODAY'S TOP 5:

☐
☐
☐
☐
☐

DWELL IN GRATITUDE:

♡
♡
♡

MASTERY & WELL-BEING:

H2O ⊔ ⊔ ⊔ ⊔ ⊔ ⊔ ⊔

EXERCISE 🏃 🏃 🏃 🏃 🏃 🏃 🏃
15 15 15 15 15 15 15

☐ DAILY HABIT

FRIDAY

TODAY'S TOP 5:

☐
☐
☐
☐
☐

DWELL IN GRATITUDE:

♡
♡
♡

MASTERY & WELL-BEING:

H2O ⊔ ⊔ ⊔ ⊔ ⊔ ⊔ ⊔

EXERCISE 🏃 🏃 🏃 🏃 🏃 🏃 🏃
15 15 15 15 15 15

☐ DAILY HABIT

SATURDAY

SUNDAY

WEEKLY REFLECTION:

How are you feeling about the progress made towards your big picture milestones this week?

What are you most proud of this week?

Are you on track for conquering the big picture milestones you set for this sprint? Could you have done anything differently?

Did you stay on top of your health and maintain your new habit?

Did you have any big insights or serendipitous moments?

FOR NEXT WEEK:

☐
☐
☐
☐
☐
☐
☐
☐
☐
☐
☐
☐
☐
☐

All we have to decide is what to do with the time that is given to us.

– GANDALF, CHARACTER IN *THE FELLOWSHIP OF THE RING* BY J. R. R. TOLKIEN, AUTHOR

MONDAY	TUESDAY	WEDNESDAY
TODAY'S TOP 5:	**TODAY'S TOP 5:**	**TODAY'S TOP 5:**
☐	☐	☐
☐	☐	☐
☐	☐	☐
☐	☐	☐
☐	☐	☐
DWELL IN GRATITUDE:	**DWELL IN GRATITUDE:**	**DWELL IN GRATITUDE:**
♡	♡	♡
♡	♡	♡
♡	♡	♡

MASTERY & WELL-BEING:	MASTERY & WELL-BEING:	MASTERY & WELL-BEING:
H2O ▯▯▯▯▯▯▯▯	H2O ▯▯▯▯▯▯▯▯	H2O ▯▯▯▯▯▯▯▯
EXERCISE 15 15 15 15 15 15	EXERCISE 15 15 15 15 15 15	EXERCISE 15 15 15 15 15 15
☐ DAILY HABIT	☐ DAILY HABIT	☐ DAILY HABIT

DELIVERABLES:

RECEIVABLES:

THURSDAY

TODAY'S TOP 5:

☐
☐
☐
☐
☐

DWELL IN GRATITUDE:

♡
♡
♡

MASTERY & WELL-BEING:

H2O 🥛🥛🥛🥛🥛🥛🥛

EXERCISE 🏃🏃🏃🏃🏃🏃🏃
15 15 15 15 15 15 15

☐ DAILY HABIT

FRIDAY

TODAY'S TOP 5:

☐
☐
☐
☐
☐

DWELL IN GRATITUDE:

♡
♡
♡

MASTERY & WELL-BEING:

H2O 🥛🥛🥛🥛🥛🥛🥛

EXERCISE 🏃🏃🏃🏃🏃🏃🏃
15 15 15 15 15 15 15

☐ DAILY HABIT

SATURDAY

SUNDAY

WEEKLY REFLECTION:

How are you feeling about the progress made towards your big picture milestones this week?

😀 😍 😊 😐 😕 😣

What are you most proud of this week?

Are you on track for conquering the big picture milestones you set for this sprint? Could you have done anything differently?

Did you stay on top of your health and maintain your new habit?

Did you have any big insights or serendipitous moments?

FOR NEXT WEEK:

☐
☐
☐
☐
☐
☐
☐
☐
☐
☐
☐
☐
☐
☐

I am...

It takes courage to grow up and turn out to be who you really are.

— E. E. CUMMINGS, POET

MONDAY	TUESDAY	WEDNESDAY

TODAY'S TOP 5:
- ☐
- ☐
- ☐
- ☐
- ☐

DWELL IN GRATITUDE:
- ♡
- ♡
- ♡

TODAY'S TOP 5:
- ☐
- ☐
- ☐
- ☐
- ☐

DWELL IN GRATITUDE:
- ♡
- ♡
- ♡

TODAY'S TOP 5:
- ☐
- ☐
- ☐
- ☐
- ☐

DWELL IN GRATITUDE:
- ♡
- ♡
- ♡

MASTERY & WELL-BEING:

H2O 🥛🥛🥛🥛🥛🥛🥛

EXERCISE 🏃🏃🏃🏃🏃🏃
15 15 15 15 15 15

☐ DAILY HABIT

MASTERY & WELL-BEING:

H2O 🥛🥛🥛🥛🥛🥛🥛

EXERCISE 🏃🏃🏃🏃🏃🏃
15 15 15 15 15 15

☐ DAILY HABIT

MASTERY & WELL-BEING:

H2O 🥛🥛🥛🥛🥛🥛🥛

EXERCISE 🏃🏃🏃🏃🏃🏃
15 15 15 15 15 15

☐ DAILY HABIT

DELIVERABLES:

RECEIVABLES:

BIG PICTURE PRIORITIES TO FOCUS ON:

DATE

THURSDAY

TODAY'S TOP 5:

- ☐
- ☐
- ☐
- ☐
- ☐

DWELL IN GRATITUDE:

- ♡
- ♡
- ♡

MASTERY & WELL-BEING:

H2O 🥛🥛🥛🥛🥛🥛🥛

EXERCISE 🏃🏃🏃🏃🏃🏃🏃
15   15   15   15   15   15   15

☐ DAILY HABIT

FRIDAY

TODAY'S TOP 5:

- ☐
- ☐
- ☐
- ☐
- ☐

DWELL IN GRATITUDE:

- ♡
- ♡
- ♡

MASTERY & WELL-BEING:

H2O 🥛🥛🥛🥛🥛🥛🥛

EXERCISE 🏃🏃🏃🏃🏃🏃🏃
15   15   15   15   15   15   15

☐ DAILY HABIT

SATURDAY

SUNDAY

WEEKLY REFLECTION:

How are you feeling about the progress made towards your big picture milestones this week?

🤑 😍 😀 😐 😟 😣

What are you most proud of this week?

Are you on track for conquering the big picture milestones you set for this sprint? Could you have done anything differently?

Did you stay on top of your health and maintain your new habit?

Did you have any big insights or serendipitous moments?

FOR NEXT WEEK:

- ☐
- ☐
- ☐
- ☐
- ☐
- ☐
- ☐
- ☐
- ☐
- ☐
- ☐
- ☐
- ☐
- ☐

If your actions create a legacy that inspires others to dream more, learn more, do more and become more, then, you are an excellent leader.

– DOLLY PARTON, SINGER-SONGWRITER

MONDAY	TUESDAY	WEDNESDAY

TODAY'S TOP 5:

☐
☐
☐
☐
☐

TODAY'S TOP 5:

☐
☐
☐
☐
☐

TODAY'S TOP 5:

☐
☐
☐
☐
☐

DWELL IN GRATITUDE:

♡
♡
♡

DWELL IN GRATITUDE:

♡
♡
♡

DWELL IN GRATITUDE:

♡
♡
♡

MASTERY & WELL-BEING:

H2O ⬜⬜⬜⬜⬜⬜⬜⬜

EXERCISE 🏃🏃🏃🏃🏃🏃
15 15 15 15 15 15

☐ DAILY HABIT

MASTERY & WELL-BEING:

H2O ⬜⬜⬜⬜⬜⬜⬜⬜

EXERCISE 🏃🏃🏃🏃🏃🏃
15 15 15 15 15 15

☐ DAILY HABIT

MASTERY & WELL-BEING:

H2O ⬜⬜⬜⬜⬜⬜⬜⬜

EXERCISE 🏃🏃🏃🏃🏃🏃
15 15 15 15 15 15

☐ DAILY HABIT

DELIVERABLES:

RECEIVABLES:

THURSDAY

TODAY'S TOP 5:

- ☐
- ☐
- ☐
- ☐
- ☐

DWELL IN GRATITUDE:

- ♡
- ♡
- ♡

MASTERY & WELL-BEING:

H2O ☐ ☐ ☐ ☐ ☐ ☐ ☐

EXERCISE 🏃 🏃 🏃 🏃 🏃 🏃 🏃
15 15 15 15 15 15 15

☐ DAILY HABIT

FRIDAY

TODAY'S TOP 5:

- ☐
- ☐
- ☐
- ☐
- ☐

DWELL IN GRATITUDE:

- ♡
- ♡
- ♡

MASTERY & WELL-BEING:

H2O ☐ ☐ ☐ ☐ ☐ ☐ ☐

EXERCISE 🏃 🏃 🏃 🏃 🏃 🏃 🏃
15 15 15 15 15 15 15

☐ DAILY HABIT

SATURDAY

SUNDAY

WEEKLY REFLECTION:

How are you feeling about the progress made towards your big picture milestones this week?

😁 😍 🙂 😐 🙁 😞

What are you most proud of this week?

Are you on track for conquering the big picture milestones you set for this sprint? Could you have done anything differently?

Did you stay on top of your health and maintain your new habit?

Did you have any big insights or serendipitous moments?

FOR NEXT WEEK:

- ☐
- ☐
- ☐
- ☐
- ☐
- ☐
- ☐
- ☐
- ☐
- ☐
- ☐
- ☐
- ☐
- ☐

I am...

There are two kinds of stones, as everyone knows, one of which rolls.

— AMELIA EARHART, AVIATOR

MONDAY	TUESDAY	WEDNESDAY

TODAY'S TOP 5:

☐
☐
☐
☐
☐

DWELL IN GRATITUDE:

♡
♡
♡

TODAY'S TOP 5:

☐
☐
☐
☐
☐

DWELL IN GRATITUDE:

♡
♡
♡

TODAY'S TOP 5:

☐
☐
☐
☐
☐

DWELL IN GRATITUDE:

♡
♡
♡

MASTERY & WELL-BEING:

H2O ▢▢▢▢▢▢▢▢

EXERCISE 🏃15 🏃15 🏃15 🏃15 🏃15 🏃15 🏃15

☐ DAILY HABIT

MASTERY & WELL-BEING:

H2O ▢▢▢▢▢▢▢▢

EXERCISE 🏃15 🏃15 🏃15 🏃15 🏃15 🏃15 🏃15

☐ DAILY HABIT

MASTERY & WELL-BEING:

H2O ▢▢▢▢▢▢▢▢

EXERCISE 🏃15 🏃15 🏃15 🏃15 🏃15 🏃15 🏃15

☐ DAILY HABIT

DELIVERABLES:

RECEIVABLES:

DATE

THURSDAY

TODAY'S TOP 5:

☐
☐
☐
☐
☐

DWELL IN GRATITUDE:

♡
♡
♡

MASTERY & WELL-BEING:

H2O ⊔ ⊔ ⊔ ⊔ ⊔ ⊔ ⊔

EXERCISE 🏃 🏃 🏃 🏃 🏃 🏃 🏃
15 15 15 15 15 15 15

☐ DAILY HABIT

FRIDAY

TODAY'S TOP 5:

☐
☐
☐
☐
☐

DWELL IN GRATITUDE:

♡
♡
♡

MASTERY & WELL-BEING:

H2O ⊔ ⊔ ⊔ ⊔ ⊔ ⊔ ⊔

EXERCISE 🏃 🏃 🏃 🏃 🏃 🏃 🏃
15 15 15 15 15 15 15

☐ DAILY HABIT

SATURDAY

SUNDAY

WEEKLY REFLECTION:

How are you feeling about the progress made towards your big picture milestones this week?

What are you most proud of this week?

Are you on track for conquering the big picture milestones you set for this sprint? Could you have done anything differently?

Did you stay on top of your health and maintain your new habit?

Did you have any big insights or serendipitous moments?

FOR NEXT WEEK:

☐
☐
☐
☐
☐
☐
☐
☐
☐
☐
☐
☐
☐
☐

I am...

*I never dreamed about success.
I worked for it.*

— ESTÉE LAUDER, BUSINESSWOMAN

MONDAY	TUESDAY	WEDNESDAY

TODAY'S TOP 5:

☐
☐
☐
☐
☐

DWELL IN GRATITUDE:

♡
♡
♡

TODAY'S TOP 5:

☐
☐
☐
☐
☐

DWELL IN GRATITUDE:

♡
♡
♡

TODAY'S TOP 5:

☐
☐
☐
☐
☐

DWELL IN GRATITUDE:

♡
♡
♡

MASTERY & WELL-BEING:

H2O ⬚⬚⬚⬚⬚⬚⬚⬚

EXERCISE 🏃🏃🏃🏃🏃🏃🏃
15 15 15 15 15 15 15

☐ DAILY HABIT

MASTERY & WELL-BEING:

H2O ⬚⬚⬚⬚⬚⬚⬚⬚

EXERCISE 🏃🏃🏃🏃🏃🏃🏃
15 15 15 15 15 15 15

☐ DAILY HABIT

MASTERY & WELL-BEING:

H2O ⬚⬚⬚⬚⬚⬚⬚⬚

EXERCISE 🏃🏃🏃🏃🏃🏃🏃
15 15 15 15 15 15 15

☐ DAILY HABIT

DELIVERABLES:

RECEIVABLES:

THURSDAY	FRIDAY	SATURDAY

TODAY'S TOP 5:

☐
☐
☐
☐
☐

TODAY'S TOP 5:

☐
☐
☐
☐
☐

DWELL IN GRATITUDE:

♡
♡
♡

DWELL IN GRATITUDE:

♡
♡
♡

SUNDAY

MASTERY & WELL-BEING:

H2O 🥛🥛🥛🥛🥛🥛🥛

EXERCISE 🏃🏃🏃🏃🏃🏃🏃
15 15 15 15 15 15 15

☐ DAILY HABIT

MASTERY & WELL-BEING:

H2O 🥛🥛🥛🥛🥛🥛🥛

EXERCISE 🏃🏃🏃🏃🏃🏃🏃
15 15 15 15 15 15 15

☐ DAILY HABIT

WEEKLY REFLECTION:

FOR NEXT WEEK:

How are you feeling about the progress made towards your big picture milestones this week?

What are you most proud of this week?

Are you on track for conquering the big picture milestones you set for this sprint? Could you have done anything differently?

Did you stay on top of your health and maintain your new habit?

Did you have any big insights or serendipitous moments?

☐
☐
☐
☐
☐
☐
☐
☐
☐
☐
☐
☐
☐
☐

I am...

If one is lucky, a solitary fantasy can totally transform one million realities.

— MAYA ANGELOU, POET

MONDAY	TUESDAY	WEDNESDAY
TODAY'S TOP 5:	**TODAY'S TOP 5:**	**TODAY'S TOP 5:**
☐	☐	☐
☐	☐	☐
☐	☐	☐
☐	☐	☐
☐	☐	☐
DWELL IN GRATITUDE:	**DWELL IN GRATITUDE:**	**DWELL IN GRATITUDE:**
♡	♡	♡
♡	♡	♡
♡	♡	♡

MASTERY & WELL-BEING:	MASTERY & WELL-BEING:	MASTERY & WELL-BEING:
H2O 〇〇〇〇〇〇〇	H2O 〇〇〇〇〇〇〇〇	H2O 〇〇〇〇〇〇〇〇
EXERCISE 🏃🏃🏃🏃🏃🏃	EXERCISE 🏃🏃🏃🏃🏃🏃	EXERCISE 🏃🏃🏃🏃🏃🏃
15 15 15 15 15 15	15 15 15 15 15 15	15 15 15 15 15 15
☐ DAILY HABIT	☐ DAILY HABIT	☐ DAILY HABIT

DELIVERABLES:

RECEIVABLES:

DATE

THURSDAY

TODAY'S TOP 5:

- [ ]
- [ ]
- [ ]
- [ ]
- [ ]

DWELL IN GRATITUDE:

♡

♡

♡

MASTERY & WELL-BEING:

H2O ⊔ ⊔ ⊔ ⊔ ⊔ ⊔ ⊔

EXERCISE 🏃 🏃 🏃 🏃 🏃 🏃 🏃
15 15 15 15 15 15 15

- [ ] DAILY HABIT

FRIDAY

TODAY'S TOP 5:

- [ ]
- [ ]
- [ ]
- [ ]
- [ ]

DWELL IN GRATITUDE:

♡

♡

♡

MASTERY & WELL-BEING:

H2O ⊔ ⊔ ⊔ ⊔ ⊔ ⊔ ⊔

EXERCISE 🏃 🏃 🏃 🏃 🏃 🏃 🏃
15 15 15 15 15 15 15

- [ ] DAILY HABIT

SATURDAY

SUNDAY

WEEKLY REFLECTION:

How are you feeling about the progress made towards your big picture milestones this week?

What are you most proud of this week?

Are you on track for conquering the big picture milestones you set for this sprint? Could you have done anything differently?

Did you stay on top of your health and maintain your new habit?

Did you have any big insights or serendipitous moments?

FOR NEXT WEEK:

- [ ]
- [ ]
- [ ]
- [ ]
- [ ]
- [ ]
- [ ]
- [ ]
- [ ]
- [ ]
- [ ]
- [ ]
- [ ]
- [ ]

Way to go! You conquered the first sprint.

What are you most proud of achieving in the last twelve weeks?

Did you accomplish your "Balanced Ambition" goals and desires?

What milestones did you conquer for your Big Picture Goals? Which ones need to be pushed back or adjusted?

How did you reward yourself for all you achieved the last twelve weeks?

How are you feeling about the new habit you cemented into your daily routine?

How do you feel about the last quarter overall?

SPRINT 2

Sprint: _____

You are worthy of every wish, dream, goal, and desire in your heart for the year ahead.

BIG PICTURE MILESTONES

1
2
3
4
5
6
7

BRAIN DUMP

List every task you can think of for each milestone above.

☐ PUT THESE INTO A PROJECT MANAGEMENT SYSTEM AND ASSIGN DEADLINES

You might be surprised by the outcome when you surrender to your goals. it might be beyond what you thought was possible.

- NATALIE MACNEIL

BALANCED AMBITION

HABIT:	LEARNING:	GIVING BACK:

HEALTH:	RELATIONSHIPS:	ADVENTURE:

CONSCIOUS CREATION

What are you creating to share your talents and gifts with the world?

BLOG POST, VIDEO OR SOCIAL MEDIA CONTENT I WANT TO CREATE	OUTLINE	DRAFT	EDIT	PUBLISH

VISUALIZATION

What will your life look like and feel like if you conquer these goals and milestones?

SPRINT REWARD

How will you reward yourself for achieving these milestones and goals?

I am...

MONDAY	TUESDAY	WEDNESDAY

TODAY'S TOP 5:

☐

☐

☐

☐

☐

DWELL IN GRATITUDE:

♡

♡

♡

TODAY'S TOP 5:

☐

☐

☐

☐

☐

DWELL IN GRATITUDE:

♡

♡

♡

TODAY'S TOP 5:

☐

☐

☐

☐

☐

DWELL IN GRATITUDE:

♡

♡

♡

MASTERY & WELL-BEING:

H2O ⊔ ⊔ ⊔ ⊔ ⊔ ⊔ ⊔

EXERCISE 15 15 15 15 15 15 15

☐ DAILY HABIT

MASTERY & WELL-BEING:

H2O ⊔ ⊔ ⊔ ⊔ ⊔ ⊔ ⊔

EXERCISE 15 15 15 15 15 15 15

☐ DAILY HABIT

MASTERY & WELL-BEING:

H2O ⊔ ⊔ ⊔ ⊔ ⊔ ⊔ ⊔

EXERCISE 15 15 15 15 15 15 15

☐ DAILY HABIT

DELIVERABLES:

RECEIVABLES:

THURSDAY

TODAY'S TOP 5:

☐
☐
☐
☐
☐

DWELL IN GRATITUDE:

♡
♡
♡

MASTERY & WELL-BEING:

H2O ⬜ ⬜ ⬜ ⬜ ⬜ ⬜ ⬜

EXERCISE 🏃 🏃 🏃 🏃 🏃 🏃 🏃
15 15 15 15 15 15 15

☐ DAILY HABIT

FRIDAY

TODAY'S TOP 5:

☐
☐
☐
☐
☐

DWELL IN GRATITUDE:

♡
♡
♡

MASTERY & WELL-BEING:

H2O ⬜ ⬜ ⬜ ⬜ ⬜ ⬜ ⬜

EXERCISE 🏃 🏃 🏃 🏃 🏃 🏃 🏃
15 15 15 15 15 15 15

☐ DAILY HABIT

SATURDAY

SUNDAY

WEEKLY REFLECTION:

How are you feeling about the progress made towards your big picture milestones this week?

😁💲 😍 😊 😐 😟 😫

What are you most proud of this week?

Are you on track for conquering the big picture milestones you set for this sprint? Could you have done anything differently?

Did you stay on top of your health and maintain your new habit?

Did you have any big insights or serendipitous moments?

FOR NEXT WEEK:

☐
☐
☐
☐
☐
☐
☐
☐
☐
☐
☐
☐
☐
☐

We are not interested in the possibilities of defeat; they do not exist.

– VICTORIA, QUEEN OF ENGLAND

MONDAY	TUESDAY	WEDNESDAY

TODAY'S TOP 5:

☐
☐
☐
☐
☐

DWELL IN GRATITUDE:

♡
♡
♡

TODAY'S TOP 5:

☐
☐
☐
☐
☐

DWELL IN GRATITUDE:

♡
♡
♡

TODAY'S TOP 5:

☐
☐
☐
☐
☐

DWELL IN GRATITUDE:

♡
♡
♡

MASTERY & WELL-BEING:

H2O ⬜⬜⬜⬜⬜⬜⬜⬜

EXERCISE 15 15 15 15 15 15 15

☐ DAILY HABIT

MASTERY & WELL-BEING:

H2O ⬜⬜⬜⬜⬜⬜⬜⬜

EXERCISE 15 15 15 15 15 15 15

☐ DAILY HABIT

MASTERY & WELL-BEING:

H2O ⬜⬜⬜⬜⬜⬜⬜⬜

EXERCISE 15 15 15 15 15 15 15

☐ DAILY HABIT

DELIVERABLES:

RECEIVABLES:

THURSDAY

TODAY'S TOP 5:

☐
☐
☐
☐
☐

DWELL IN GRATITUDE:

♡
♡
♡

MASTERY & WELL-BEING:

H2O 🥛🥛🥛🥛🥛🥛🥛

EXERCISE 🏃🏃🏃🏃🏃🏃🏃
       15 15 15 15 15 15 15

☐ DAILY HABIT

FRIDAY

TODAY'S TOP 5:

☐
☐
☐
☐
☐

DWELL IN GRATITUDE:

♡
♡
♡

MASTERY & WELL-BEING:

H2O 🥛🥛🥛🥛🥛🥛🥛

EXERCISE 🏃🏃🏃🏃🏃🏃🏃
       15 15 15 15 15 15 15

☐ DAILY HABIT

SATURDAY

SUNDAY

WEEKLY REFLECTION:

How are you feeling about the progress made towards your big picture milestones this week?

😁 😍 😃 😐 😟 😫

What are you most proud of this week?

Are you on track for conquering the big picture milestones you set for this sprint? Could you have done anything differently?

Did you stay on top of your health and maintain your new habit?

Did you have any big insights or serendipitous moments?

FOR NEXT WEEK:

☐
☐
☐
☐
☐
☐
☐
☐
☐
☐
☐
☐
☐
☐

I am...

My philosophy is that not only are you responsible for your life, but doing the best at this moment puts you in the best place for the next moment.

– OPRAH WINFREY, ENTREPRENEUR

MONDAY	TUESDAY	WEDNESDAY

TODAY'S TOP 5:

☐
☐
☐
☐
☐

DWELL IN GRATITUDE:

♡
♡
♡

TODAY'S TOP 5:

☐
☐
☐
☐
☐

DWELL IN GRATITUDE:

♡
♡
♡

TODAY'S TOP 5:

☐
☐
☐
☐
☐

DWELL IN GRATITUDE:

♡
♡
♡

MASTERY & WELL-BEING:

H2O ⊔ ⊔ ⊔ ⊔ ⊔ ⊔ ⊔ ⊔

EXERCISE 🏃 🏃 🏃 🏃 🏃 🏃 🏃
      15 15 15 15 15 15 15

☐ DAILY HABIT

MASTERY & WELL-BEING:

H2O ⊔ ⊔ ⊔ ⊔ ⊔ ⊔ ⊔ ⊔

EXERCISE 🏃 🏃 🏃 🏃 🏃 🏃 🏃
      15 15 15 15 15 15 15

☐ DAILY HABIT

MASTERY & WELL-BEING:

H2O ⊔ ⊔ ⊔ ⊔ ⊔ ⊔ ⊔ ⊔

EXERCISE 🏃 🏃 🏃 🏃 🏃 🏃 🏃
      15 15 15 15 15 15 15

☐ DAILY HABIT

DELIVERABLES:

RECEIVABLES:

BIG PICTURE PRIORITIES TO FOCUS ON:

DATE

THURSDAY

TODAY'S TOP 5:

- [ ]
- [ ]
- [ ]
- [ ]
- [ ]

DWELL IN GRATITUDE:

♡
♡
♡

MASTERY & WELL-BEING:

H2O 🥛🥛🥛🥛🥛🥛🥛🥛

EXERCISE 🏃🏃🏃🏃🏃🏃🏃
15 15 15 15 15 15 15

- [ ] DAILY HABIT

FRIDAY

TODAY'S TOP 5:

- [ ]
- [ ]
- [ ]
- [ ]
- [ ]

DWELL IN GRATITUDE:

♡
♡
♡

MASTERY & WELL-BEING:

H2O 🥛🥛🥛🥛🥛🥛🥛🥛

EXERCISE 🏃🏃🏃🏃🏃🏃🏃
15 15 15 15 15 15 15

- [ ] DAILY HABIT

SATURDAY

SUNDAY

WEEKLY REFLECTION:

How are you feeling about the progress made towards your big picture milestones this week?

What are you most proud of this week?

Are you on track for conquering the big picture milestones you set for this sprint? Could you have done anything differently?

Did you stay on top of your health and maintain your new habit?

Did you have any big insights or serendipitous moments?

FOR NEXT WEEK:

- [ ]
- [ ]
- [ ]
- [ ]
- [ ]
- [ ]
- [ ]
- [ ]
- [ ]
- [ ]
- [ ]
- [ ]
- [ ]
- [ ]

I am...

MONDAY	TUESDAY	WEDNESDAY

TODAY'S TOP 5:

☐
☐
☐
☐
☐

DWELL IN GRATITUDE:

♡
♡
♡

TODAY'S TOP 5:

☐
☐
☐
☐
☐

DWELL IN GRATITUDE:

♡
♡
♡

TODAY'S TOP 5:

☐
☐
☐
☐
☐

DWELL IN GRATITUDE:

♡
♡
♡

MASTERY & WELL-BEING:

H2O ⊔ ⊔ ⊔ ⊔ ⊔ ⊔ ⊔ ⊔

EXERCISE 🏃 🏃 🏃 🏃 🏃 🏃 🏃
15 15 15 15 15 15 15

☐ DAILY HABIT

MASTERY & WELL-BEING:

H2O ⊔ ⊔ ⊔ ⊔ ⊔ ⊔ ⊔ ⊔

EXERCISE 🏃 🏃 🏃 🏃 🏃 🏃 🏃
15 15 15 15 15 15 15

☐ DAILY HABIT

MASTERY & WELL-BEING:

H2O ⊔ ⊔ ⊔ ⊔ ⊔ ⊔ ⊔ ⊔

EXERCISE 🏃 🏃 🏃 🏃 🏃 🏃 🏃
15 15 15 15 15 15 15

☐ DAILY HABIT

DELIVERABLES:

RECEIVABLES:

BIG PICTURE PRIORITIES TO FOCUS ON:

DATE

THURSDAY

TODAY'S TOP 5:

- [ ]
- [ ]
- [ ]
- [ ]
- [ ]

DWELL IN GRATITUDE:

♡

♡

♡

MASTERY & WELL-BEING:

H2O 🥛🥛🥛🥛🥛🥛🥛

EXERCISE 🏃🏃🏃🏃🏃🏃🏃
15 15 15 15 15 15 15

- [ ] DAILY HABIT

FRIDAY

TODAY'S TOP 5:

- [ ]
- [ ]
- [ ]
- [ ]
- [ ]

DWELL IN GRATITUDE:

♡

♡

♡

MASTERY & WELL-BEING:

H2O 🥛🥛🥛🥛🥛🥛🥛

EXERCISE 🏃🏃🏃🏃🏃🏃🏃
15 15 15 15 15 15 15

- [ ] DAILY HABIT

SATURDAY

SUNDAY

WEEKLY REFLECTION:

How are you feeling about the progress made towards your big picture milestones this week?

😁 😍 🙂 😐 🙁 😟

What are you most proud of this week?

Are you on track for conquering the big picture milestones you set for this sprint? Could you have done anything differently?

Did you stay on top of your health and maintain your new habit?

Did you have any big insights or serendipitous moments?

FOR NEXT WEEK:

- [ ]
- [ ]
- [ ]
- [ ]
- [ ]
- [ ]
- [ ]
- [ ]
- [ ]
- [ ]
- [ ]
- [ ]
- [ ]
- [ ]

I am...

MONDAY	TUESDAY	WEDNESDAY

TODAY'S TOP 5:

☐
☐
☐
☐
☐

DWELL IN GRATITUDE:

♡
♡
♡

MASTERY & WELL-BEING:

H2O ⊔ ⊔ ⊔ ⊔ ⊔ ⊔ ⊔ ⊔

EXERCISE 🏃 🏃 🏃 🏃 🏃 🏃 🏃
15 15 15 15 15 15 15

☐ DAILY HABIT

TODAY'S TOP 5:

☐
☐
☐
☐
☐

DWELL IN GRATITUDE:

♡
♡
♡

MASTERY & WELL-BEING:

H2O ⊔ ⊔ ⊔ ⊔ ⊔ ⊔ ⊔ ⊔

EXERCISE 🏃 🏃 🏃 🏃 🏃 🏃 🏃
15 15 15 15 15 15 15

☐ DAILY HABIT

TODAY'S TOP 5:

☐
☐
☐
☐
☐

DWELL IN GRATITUDE:

♡
♡
♡

MASTERY & WELL-BEING:

H2O ⊔ ⊔ ⊔ ⊔ ⊔ ⊔ ⊔ ⊔

EXERCISE 🏃 🏃 🏃 🏃 🏃 🏃 🏃
15 15 15 15 15 15 15

☐ DAILY HABIT

DELIVERABLES:

RECEIVABLES:

THURSDAY

TODAY'S TOP 5:

- [ ]
- [ ]
- [ ]
- [ ]
- [ ]

DWELL IN GRATITUDE:

♡
♡
♡

MASTERY & WELL-BEING:

H2O 🥛🥛🥛🥛🥛🥛🥛

EXERCISE 🏃🏃🏃🏃🏃🏃🏃
　　　　15　15　15　15　15　15　15

- [ ] DAILY HABIT

FRIDAY

TODAY'S TOP 5:

- [ ]
- [ ]
- [ ]
- [ ]
- [ ]

DWELL IN GRATITUDE:

♡
♡
♡

MASTERY & WELL-BEING:

H2O 🥛🥛🥛🥛🥛🥛🥛

EXERCISE 🏃🏃🏃🏃🏃🏃🏃
　　　　15　15　15　15　15　15　15

- [ ] DAILY HABIT

SATURDAY

SUNDAY

WEEKLY REFLECTION:

How are you feeling about the progress made towards your big picture milestones this week?

😁 😍 😃 😐 😒 😣

What are you most proud of this week?

Are you on track for conquering the big picture milestones you set for this sprint? Could you have done anything differently?

Did you stay on top of your health and maintain your new habit?

Did you have any big insights or serendipitous moments?

FOR NEXT WEEK:

- [ ]
- [ ]
- [ ]
- [ ]
- [ ]
- [ ]
- [ ]
- [ ]
- [ ]
- [ ]
- [ ]
- [ ]
- [ ]
- [ ]

I am...

Don't waste a single second. Just move forward as fast as you can, and go for it.
– REBECCA WOODCOCK,
CO-FOUNDER OF CAKEHEALTH

MONDAY	TUESDAY	WEDNESDAY
TODAY'S TOP 5:	TODAY'S TOP 5:	TODAY'S TOP 5:
☐	☐	☐
☐	☐	☐
☐	☐	☐
☐	☐	☐
☐	☐	☐
DWELL IN GRATITUDE:	DWELL IN GRATITUDE:	DWELL IN GRATITUDE:
♡	♡	♡
♡	♡	♡
♡	♡	♡
MASTERY & WELL-BEING:	**MASTERY & WELL-BEING:**	**MASTERY & WELL-BEING:**
H2O ☐☐☐☐☐☐☐	H2O ☐☐☐☐☐☐☐	H2O ☐☐☐☐☐☐☐
EXERCISE 🏃🏃🏃🏃🏃🏃🏃 15 15 15 15 15 15 15	EXERCISE 🏃🏃🏃🏃🏃🏃🏃 15 15 15 15 15 15 15	EXERCISE 🏃🏃🏃🏃🏃🏃🏃 15 15 15 15 15 15 15
☐ DAILY HABIT	☐ DAILY HABIT	☐ DAILY HABIT

DELIVERABLES:

RECEIVABLES:

THURSDAY

TODAY'S TOP 5:

☐

☐

☐

☐

☐

DWELL IN GRATITUDE:

♡

♡

♡

MASTERY & WELL-BEING:

H2O ⊔ ⊔ ⊔ ⊔ ⊔ ⊔ ⊔

EXERCISE 🏃 🏃 🏃 🏃 🏃 🏃 🏃
15 15 15 15 15 15 15

☐ DAILY HABIT

FRIDAY

TODAY'S TOP 5:

☐

☐

☐

☐

☐

DWELL IN GRATITUDE:

♡

♡

♡

MASTERY & WELL-BEING:

H2O ⊔ ⊔ ⊔ ⊔ ⊔ ⊔ ⊔

EXERCISE 🏃 🏃 🏃 🏃 🏃 🏃 🏃
15 15 15 15 15 15 15

☐ DAILY HABIT

SATURDAY

SUNDAY

WEEKLY REFLECTION:

How are you feeling about the progress made towards your big picture milestones this week?

What are you most proud of this week?

Are you on track for conquering the big picture milestones you set for this sprint? Could you have done anything differently?

Did you stay on top of your health and maintain your new habit?

Did you have any big insights or serendipitous moments?

FOR NEXT WEEK:

☐

☐

☐

☐

☐

☐

☐

☐

☐

☐

☐

☐

☐

☐

I am...

I choose to make the rest of my life the best of my life.

– LOUISE HAY, AUTHOR

MONDAY	TUESDAY	WEDNESDAY

TODAY'S TOP 5:

☐
☐
☐
☐
☐

DWELL IN GRATITUDE:

♡
♡
♡

TODAY'S TOP 5:

☐
☐
☐
☐
☐

DWELL IN GRATITUDE:

♡
♡
♡

TODAY'S TOP 5:

☐
☐
☐
☐
☐

DWELL IN GRATITUDE:

♡
♡
♡

MASTERY & WELL-BEING:

H2O ⬚ ⬚ ⬚ ⬚ ⬚ ⬚ ⬚

EXERCISE 🏃 🏃 🏃 🏃 🏃 🏃
15 15 15 15 15 15

☐ DAILY HABIT

MASTERY & WELL-BEING:

H2O ⬚ ⬚ ⬚ ⬚ ⬚ ⬚ ⬚

EXERCISE 🏃 🏃 🏃 🏃 🏃 🏃
15 15 15 15 15 15

☐ DAILY HABIT

MASTERY & WELL-BEING:

H2O ⬚ ⬚ ⬚ ⬚ ⬚ ⬚ ⬚

EXERCISE 🏃 🏃 🏃 🏃 🏃 🏃
15 15 15 15 15 15

☐ DAILY HABIT

DELIVERABLES:

RECEIVABLES:

THURSDAY

TODAY'S TOP 5:

☐
☐
☐
☐
☐

DWELL IN GRATITUDE:

♡
♡
♡

MASTERY & WELL-BEING:

H2O ▯▯▯▯▯▯▯

EXERCISE 🏃🏃🏃🏃🏃🏃🏃
       15 15 15 15 15 15 15

☐ DAILY HABIT

FRIDAY

TODAY'S TOP 5:

☐
☐
☐
☐
☐

DWELL IN GRATITUDE:

♡
♡
♡

MASTERY & WELL-BEING:

H2O ▯▯▯▯▯▯▯

EXERCISE 🏃🏃🏃🏃🏃🏃🏃
       15 15 15 15 15 15 15

☐ DAILY HABIT

SATURDAY

SUNDAY

WEEKLY REFLECTION:

How are you feeling about the progress made towards your big picture milestones this week?

What are you most proud of this week?

Are you on track for conquering the big picture milestones you set for this sprint? Could you have done anything differently?

Did you stay on top of your health and maintain your new habit?

Did you have any big insights or serendipitous moments?

FOR NEXT WEEK:

☐
☐
☐
☐
☐
☐
☐
☐
☐
☐
☐
☐
☐
☐

I am...

MONDAY	TUESDAY	WEDNESDAY

TODAY'S TOP 5:

☐
☐
☐
☐
☐

TODAY'S TOP 5:

☐
☐
☐
☐
☐

TODAY'S TOP 5:

☐
☐
☐
☐
☐

DWELL IN GRATITUDE:

♡
♡
♡

DWELL IN GRATITUDE:

♡
♡
♡

DWELL IN GRATITUDE:

♡
♡
♡

MASTERY & WELL-BEING:

H2O ⬜⬜⬜⬜⬜⬜⬜⬜

EXERCISE 🏃🏃🏃🏃🏃🏃🏃
15 15 15 15 15 15 15

☐ DAILY HABIT

MASTERY & WELL-BEING:

H2O ⬜⬜⬜⬜⬜⬜⬜⬜

EXERCISE 🏃🏃🏃🏃🏃🏃🏃
15 15 15 15 15 15 15

☐ DAILY HABIT

MASTERY & WELL-BEING:

H2O ⬜⬜⬜⬜⬜⬜⬜⬜

EXERCISE 🏃🏃🏃🏃🏃🏃🏃
15 15 15 15 15 15 15

☐ DAILY HABIT

DELIVERABLES:

RECEIVABLES:

THURSDAY

TODAY'S TOP 5:

- [ ]
- [ ]
- [ ]
- [ ]
- [ ]

DWELL IN GRATITUDE:

♡
♡
♡

MASTERY & WELL-BEING:

H2O ⊔ ⊔ ⊔ ⊔ ⊔ ⊔ ⊔

EXERCISE 🏃 🏃 🏃 🏃 🏃 🏃 🏃
15 15 15 15 15 15 15

- [ ] DAILY HABIT

FRIDAY

TODAY'S TOP 5:

- [ ]
- [ ]
- [ ]
- [ ]
- [ ]

DWELL IN GRATITUDE:

♡
♡
♡

MASTERY & WELL-BEING:

H2O ⊔ ⊔ ⊔ ⊔ ⊔ ⊔ ⊔

EXERCISE 🏃 🏃 🏃 🏃 🏃 🏃 🏃
15 15 15 15 15 15 15

- [ ] DAILY HABIT

SATURDAY

SUNDAY

WEEKLY REFLECTION:

How are you feeling about the progress made towards your big picture milestones this week?

😁 😍 🙂 😐 🙁 ☹️

What are you most proud of this week?

Are you on track for conquering the big picture milestones you set for this sprint? Could you have done anything differently?

Did you stay on top of your health and maintain your new habit?

Did you have any big insights or serendipitous moments?

FOR NEXT WEEK:

- [ ]
- [ ]
- [ ]
- [ ]
- [ ]
- [ ]
- [ ]
- [ ]
- [ ]
- [ ]
- [ ]
- [ ]
- [ ]

True leadership stems from individuality that is honestly and sometimes imperfectly expressed.

— SHERYL SANDBERG, COO OF FACEBOOK

MONDAY	TUESDAY	WEDNESDAY
TODAY'S TOP 5:	**TODAY'S TOP 5:**	**TODAY'S TOP 5:**
☐	☐	☐
☐	☐	☐
☐	☐	☐
☐	☐	☐
☐	☐	☐
DWELL IN GRATITUDE:	**DWELL IN GRATITUDE:**	**DWELL IN GRATITUDE:**
♡	♡	♡
♡	♡	♡
♡	♡	♡
MASTERY & WELL-BEING:	**MASTERY & WELL-BEING:**	**MASTERY & WELL-BEING:**
H2O ▯▯▯▯▯▯▯▯	H2O ▯▯▯▯▯▯▯▯	H2O ▯▯▯▯▯▯▯▯
EXERCISE 🏃🏃🏃🏃🏃🏃🏃 15 15 15 15 15 15	EXERCISE 🏃🏃🏃🏃🏃🏃🏃 15 15 15 15 15 15	EXERCISE 🏃🏃🏃🏃🏃🏃🏃 15 15 15 15 15 15
☐ DAILY HABIT	☐ DAILY HABIT	☐ DAILY HABIT

DELIVERABLES:

RECEIVABLES:

DATE

THURSDAY

TODAY'S TOP 5:

☐
☐
☐
☐
☐

DWELL IN GRATITUDE:

♡
♡
♡

MASTERY & WELL-BEING:

H2O ☐ ☐ ☐ ☐ ☐ ☐ ☐

EXERCISE 🏃 🏃 🏃 🏃 🏃 🏃 🏃
15 15 15 15 15 15 15

☐ DAILY HABIT

FRIDAY

TODAY'S TOP 5:

☐
☐
☐
☐
☐

DWELL IN GRATITUDE:

♡
♡
♡

MASTERY & WELL-BEING:

H2O ☐ ☐ ☐ ☐ ☐ ☐ ☐

EXERCISE 🏃 🏃 🏃 🏃 🏃 🏃 🏃
15 15 15 15 15 15 15

☐ DAILY HABIT

SATURDAY

SUNDAY

WEEKLY REFLECTION:

How are you feeling about the progress made towards your big picture milestones this week?

😁 😍 😊 😐 ☹️ 😣

What are you most proud of this week?

Are you on track for conquering the big picture milestones you set for this sprint? Could you have done anything differently?

Did you stay on top of your health and maintain your new habit?

Did you have any big insights or serendipitous moments?

FOR NEXT WEEK:

☐
☐
☐
☐
☐
☐
☐
☐
☐
☐
☐
☐
☐
☐

I am...

I'd rather regret the things I've done than regret the things I haven't done.

– LUCILLE BALL, ACTOR

MONDAY	TUESDAY	WEDNESDAY
TODAY'S TOP 5:	TODAY'S TOP 5:	TODAY'S TOP 5:
☐	☐	☐
☐	☐	☐
☐	☐	☐
☐	☐	☐
☐	☐	☐
DWELL IN GRATITUDE:	DWELL IN GRATITUDE:	DWELL IN GRATITUDE:
♡	♡	♡
♡	♡	♡
♡	♡	♡
MASTERY & WELL-BEING:	MASTERY & WELL-BEING:	MASTERY & WELL-BEING:
H2O	H2O	H2O
EXERCISE 15 15 15 15 15 15 15	EXERCISE 15 15 15 15 15 15 15	EXERCISE 15 15 15 15 15 15 15
☐ DAILY HABIT	☐ DAILY HABIT	☐ DAILY HABIT

DELIVERABLES:

RECEIVABLES:

BIG PICTURE PRIORITIES TO FOCUS ON:

DATE

THURSDAY	FRIDAY	SATURDAY

THURSDAY

TODAY'S TOP 5:
- ☐
- ☐
- ☐
- ☐
- ☐

DWELL IN GRATITUDE:
- ♡
- ♡
- ♡

MASTERY & WELL-BEING:

H2O ⬜⬜⬜⬜⬜⬜⬜

EXERCISE 🏃15 🏃15 🏃15 🏃15 🏃15 🏃15 🏃15

☐ DAILY HABIT

FRIDAY

TODAY'S TOP 5:
- ☐
- ☐
- ☐
- ☐
- ☐

DWELL IN GRATITUDE:
- ♡
- ♡
- ♡

MASTERY & WELL-BEING:

H2O ⬜⬜⬜⬜⬜⬜⬜

EXERCISE 🏃15 🏃15 🏃15 🏃15 🏃15 🏃15 🏃15

☐ DAILY HABIT

SATURDAY

SUNDAY

WEEKLY REFLECTION:

How are you feeling about the progress made towards your big picture milestones this week?

😁 😍 😊 😐 😟 ☹️

What are you most proud of this week?

Are you on track for conquering the big picture milestones you set for this sprint? Could you have done anything differently?

Did you stay on top of your health and maintain your new habit?

Did you have any big insights or serendipitous moments?

FOR NEXT WEEK:

- ☐
- ☐
- ☐
- ☐
- ☐
- ☐
- ☐
- ☐
- ☐
- ☐
- ☐
- ☐
- ☐
- ☐

I am...

MONDAY	TUESDAY	WEDNESDAY
TODAY'S TOP 5:	**TODAY'S TOP 5:**	**TODAY'S TOP 5:**
☐	☐	☐
☐	☐	☐
☐	☐	☐
☐	☐	☐
☐	☐	☐
DWELL IN GRATITUDE:	**DWELL IN GRATITUDE:**	**DWELL IN GRATITUDE:**
♡	♡	♡
♡	♡	♡
♡	♡	♡

MASTERY & WELL-BEING:	MASTERY & WELL-BEING:	MASTERY & WELL-BEING:
H2O ⬜⬜⬜⬜⬜⬜⬜⬜	H2O ⬜⬜⬜⬜⬜⬜⬜⬜	H2O ⬜⬜⬜⬜⬜⬜⬜⬜
EXERCISE 15 15 15 15 15 15 15	EXERCISE 15 15 15 15 15 15 15	EXERCISE 15 15 15 15 15 15 15
☐ DAILY HABIT	☐ DAILY HABIT	☐ DAILY HABIT

DELIVERABLES:

RECEIVABLES:

THURSDAY

TODAY'S TOP 5:

☐
☐
☐
☐
☐

DWELL IN GRATITUDE:

♡
♡
♡

MASTERY & WELL-BEING:

H2O ⊔ ⊔ ⊔ ⊔ ⊔ ⊔ ⊔

EXERCISE 🏃 🏃 🏃 🏃 🏃 🏃
15 15 15 15 15 15

☐ DAILY HABIT

FRIDAY

TODAY'S TOP 5:

☐
☐
☐
☐
☐

DWELL IN GRATITUDE:

♡
♡
♡

MASTERY & WELL-BEING:

H2O ⊔ ⊔ ⊔ ⊔ ⊔ ⊔ ⊔

EXERCISE 🏃 🏃 🏃 🏃 🏃 🏃
15 15 15 15 15 15

☐ DAILY HABIT

SATURDAY

SUNDAY

WEEKLY REFLECTION:

How are you feeling about the progress made towards your big picture milestones this week?

😁 😍 😊 😐 😟 😞

What are you most proud of this week?

Are you on track for conquering the big picture milestones you set for this sprint? Could you have done anything differently?

Did you stay on top of your health and maintain your new habit?

Did you have any big insights or serendipitous moments?

FOR NEXT WEEK:

☐
☐
☐
☐
☐
☐
☐
☐
☐
☐
☐
☐
☐
☐

I am...

*I learned to always take on things I'd never done before.
Growth and comfort do not coexist.*

— GINNI ROMETTY, CEO OF IBM

MONDAY	TUESDAY	WEDNESDAY
TODAY'S TOP 5:	**TODAY'S TOP 5:**	**TODAY'S TOP 5:**
☐	☐	☐
☐	☐	☐
☐	☐	☐
☐	☐	☐
☐	☐	☐
DWELL IN GRATITUDE:	**DWELL IN GRATITUDE:**	**DWELL IN GRATITUDE:**
♡	♡	♡
♡	♡	♡
♡	♡	♡
MASTERY & WELL-BEING:	**MASTERY & WELL-BEING:**	**MASTERY & WELL-BEING:**
H2O ▯▯▯▯▯▯▯▯	H2O ▯▯▯▯▯▯▯▯	H2O ▯▯▯▯▯▯▯▯
EXERCISE 15 15 15 15 15 15	EXERCISE 15 15 15 15 15 15	EXERCISE 15 15 15 15 15 15
☐ DAILY HABIT	☐ DAILY HABIT	☐ DAILY HABIT

DELIVERABLES:

RECEIVABLES:

THURSDAY

TODAY'S TOP 5:

- ☐
- ☐
- ☐
- ☐
- ☐

DWELL IN GRATITUDE:

♡
♡
♡

MASTERY & WELL-BEING:

H2O ⊔ ⊔ ⊔ ⊔ ⊔ ⊔ ⊔

EXERCISE 🏃 🏃 🏃 🏃 🏃 🏃 🏃
15 15 15 15 15 15 15

☐ DAILY HABIT

FRIDAY

TODAY'S TOP 5:

- ☐
- ☐
- ☐
- ☐
- ☐

DWELL IN GRATITUDE:

♡
♡
♡

MASTERY & WELL-BEING:

H2O ⊔ ⊔ ⊔ ⊔ ⊔ ⊔ ⊔

EXERCISE 🏃 🏃 🏃 🏃 🏃 🏃 🏃
15 15 15 15 15 15 15

☐ DAILY HABIT

SATURDAY

SUNDAY

WEEKLY REFLECTION:

How are you feeling about the progress made towards your big picture milestones this week?

What are you most proud of this week?

Are you on track for conquering the big picture milestones you set for this sprint? Could you have done anything differently?

Did you stay on top of your health and maintain your new habit?

Did you have any big insights or serendipitous moments?

FOR NEXT WEEK:

- ☐
- ☐
- ☐
- ☐
- ☐
- ☐
- ☐
- ☐
- ☐
- ☐
- ☐
- ☐
- ☐
- ☐

You're halfway there. That's a wrap on sprint two!

REFLECTION:

What are you most proud of achieving in the last twelve weeks?

Did you accomplish your "Balanced Ambition" goals and desires?

What milestones did you conquer for your Big Picture Goals? Which ones need to be pushed back or adjusted?

How did you reward yourself for all you achieved the last twelve weeks?

How are you feeling about the new habit you cemented into your daily routine?

How do you feel about the last quarter overall?

SPRINT 3

Sprint: _____

You are worthy of every wish, dream, goal, and desire in your heart for the year ahead.

BIG PICTURE MILESTONES

1
2
3
4
5
6
7

BRAIN DUMP

List every task you can think of for each milestone above.

☐ **PUT THESE INTO A PROJECT MANAGEMENT SYSTEM AND ASSIGN DEADLINES**

You can do everything you've planned because everything you'll ever need is within you.

- NATALIE MACNEIL

BALANCED AMBITION

HABIT:

LEARNING:

GIVING BACK:

HEALTH:

RELATIONSHIPS:

ADVENTURE:

CONSCIOUS CREATION

What are you creating to share your talents and gifts with the world?

BLOG POST, VIDEO OR SOCIAL MEDIA CONTENT I WANT TO CREATE	OUTLINE	DRAFT	EDIT	PUBLISH

VISUALIZATION

What will your life look like and feel like if you conquer these goals and milestones?

SPRINT REWARD

How will you reward yourself for achieving these milestones and goals?

I am...

Define success on your own terms, achieve it by your own rules, and build a life you're proud to live.

– ANNE SWEENEY, BUSINESSWOMAN

MONDAY	TUESDAY	WEDNESDAY
TODAY'S TOP 5:	TODAY'S TOP 5:	TODAY'S TOP 5:
☐	☐	☐
☐	☐	☐
☐	☐	☐
☐	☐	☐
☐	☐	☐
DWELL IN GRATITUDE:	DWELL IN GRATITUDE:	DWELL IN GRATITUDE:
♡	♡	♡
♡	♡	♡
♡	♡	♡
MASTERY & WELL-BEING:	MASTERY & WELL-BEING:	MASTERY & WELL-BEING:
H2O ⬜⬜⬜⬜⬜⬜⬜⬜	H2O ⬜⬜⬜⬜⬜⬜⬜⬜	H2O ⬜⬜⬜⬜⬜⬜⬜⬜
EXERCISE 15 15 15 15 15 15 15	EXERCISE 15 15 15 15 15 15 15	EXERCISE 15 15 15 15 15 15 15
☐ DAILY HABIT	☐ DAILY HABIT	☐ DAILY HABIT

DELIVERABLES:

RECEIVABLES:

THURSDAY

TODAY'S TOP 5:

☐
☐
☐
☐
☐

DWELL IN GRATITUDE:

♡
♡
♡

MASTERY & WELL-BEING:

H2O ⊔ ⊔ ⊔ ⊔ ⊔ ⊔ ⊔

EXERCISE 🏃 🏃 🏃 🏃 🏃 🏃 🏃
15 15 15 15 15 15 15

☐ DAILY HABIT

FRIDAY

TODAY'S TOP 5:

☐
☐
☐
☐
☐

DWELL IN GRATITUDE:

♡
♡
♡

MASTERY & WELL-BEING:

H2O ⊔ ⊔ ⊔ ⊔ ⊔ ⊔ ⊔

EXERCISE 🏃 🏃 🏃 🏃 🏃 🏃 🏃
15 15 15 15 15 15 15

☐ DAILY HABIT

SATURDAY

SUNDAY

WEEKLY REFLECTION:

How are you feeling about the progress made towards your big picture milestones this week?

😁 😍 🙂 😐 🙁 ☹️

What are you most proud of this week?

Are you on track for conquering the big picture milestones you set for this sprint? Could you have done anything differently?

Did you stay on top of your health and maintain your new habit?

Did you have any big insights or serendipitous moments?

FOR NEXT WEEK:

☐
☐
☐
☐
☐
☐
☐
☐
☐
☐
☐
☐
☐
☐

INTENTION FOR THIS WEEK:

I am...

*Power's not given to you.
You have to take it.*

– BEYONCÉ, SINGER-SONGWRITER

MONDAY	TUESDAY	WEDNESDAY

TODAY'S TOP 5:

☐
☐
☐
☐
☐

DWELL IN GRATITUDE:

♡
♡
♡

TODAY'S TOP 5:

☐
☐
☐
☐
☐

DWELL IN GRATITUDE:

♡
♡
♡

TODAY'S TOP 5:

☐
☐
☐
☐
☐

DWELL IN GRATITUDE:

♡
♡
♡

MASTERY & WELL-BEING:

H2O 🥛🥛🥛🥛🥛🥛🥛

EXERCISE 🏃🏃🏃🏃🏃🏃🏃
15 15 15 15 15 15 15

☐ DAILY HABIT

MASTERY & WELL-BEING:

H2O 🥛🥛🥛🥛🥛🥛🥛

EXERCISE 🏃🏃🏃🏃🏃🏃🏃
15 15 15 15 15 15 15

☐ DAILY HABIT

MASTERY & WELL-BEING:

H2O 🥛🥛🥛🥛🥛🥛🥛

EXERCISE 🏃🏃🏃🏃🏃🏃🏃
15 15 15 15 15 15 15

☐ DAILY HABIT

DELIVERABLES:

RECEIVABLES:

BIG PICTURE PRIORITIES TO FOCUS ON:

DATE

THURSDAY

TODAY'S TOP 5:

- [ ]
- [ ]
- [ ]
- [ ]
- [ ]

DWELL IN GRATITUDE:

♡
♡
♡

MASTERY & WELL-BEING:

H2O 🥛🥛🥛🥛🥛🥛🥛

EXERCISE 🏃🏃🏃🏃🏃🏃
15　15　15　15　15　15

- [ ] DAILY HABIT

FRIDAY

TODAY'S TOP 5:

- [ ]
- [ ]
- [ ]
- [ ]
- [ ]

DWELL IN GRATITUDE:

♡
♡
♡

MASTERY & WELL-BEING:

H2O 🥛🥛🥛🥛🥛🥛🥛

EXERCISE 🏃🏃🏃🏃🏃🏃
15　15　15　15　15　15

- [ ] DAILY HABIT

SATURDAY

SUNDAY

WEEKLY REFLECTION:

How are you feeling about the progress made towards your big picture milestones this week?

What are you most proud of this week?

Are you on track for conquering the big picture milestones you set for this sprint? Could you have done anything differently?

Did you stay on top of your health and maintain your new habit?

Did you have any big insights or serendipitous moments?

FOR NEXT WEEK:

- [ ]
- [ ]
- [ ]
- [ ]
- [ ]
- [ ]
- [ ]
- [ ]
- [ ]
- [ ]
- [ ]
- [ ]
- [ ]
- [ ]

It is our choices that show what we truly are, far more than our abilities.

— DUMBLEDORE, CHARACTER IN *HARRY POTTER AND THE CHAMBER OF SECRETS*, J. K. ROWLING, AUTHOR

MONDAY	TUESDAY	WEDNESDAY
TODAY'S TOP 5:	**TODAY'S TOP 5:**	**TODAY'S TOP 5:**
☐	☐	☐
☐	☐	☐
☐	☐	☐
☐	☐	☐
☐	☐	☐
DWELL IN GRATITUDE:	**DWELL IN GRATITUDE:**	**DWELL IN GRATITUDE:**
♡	♡	♡
♡	♡	♡
♡	♡	♡

MASTERY & WELL-BEING:	MASTERY & WELL-BEING:	MASTERY & WELL-BEING:
H2O ☐☐☐☐☐☐☐☐	H2O ☐☐☐☐☐☐☐☐	H2O ☐☐☐☐☐☐☐☐
EXERCISE 🏃🏃🏃🏃🏃🏃 15 15 15 15 15 15	EXERCISE 🏃🏃🏃🏃🏃🏃 15 15 15 15 15 15	EXERCISE 🏃🏃🏃🏃🏃🏃 15 15 15 15 15 15
☐ DAILY HABIT	☐ DAILY HABIT	☐ DAILY HABIT

DELIVERABLES:

RECEIVABLES:

THURSDAY

TODAY'S TOP 5:

☐
☐
☐
☐
☐

DWELL IN GRATITUDE:

♡
♡
♡

MASTERY & WELL-BEING:

H2O 🥛🥛🥛🥛🥛🥛🥛

EXERCISE 🏃15 🏃15 🏃15 🏃15 🏃15 🏃15

☐ DAILY HABIT

FRIDAY

TODAY'S TOP 5:

☐
☐
☐
☐
☐

DWELL IN GRATITUDE:

♡
♡
♡

MASTERY & WELL-BEING:

H2O 🥛🥛🥛🥛🥛🥛🥛

EXERCISE 🏃15 🏃15 🏃15 🏃15 🏃15 🏃15

☐ DAILY HABIT

SATURDAY

SUNDAY

WEEKLY REFLECTION:

How are you feeling about the progress made towards your big picture milestones this week?

😁 😍 😊 😐 😟 😣

What are you most proud of this week?

Are you on track for conquering the big picture milestones you set for this sprint? Could you have done anything differently?

Did you stay on top of your health and maintain your new habit?

Did you have any big insights or serendipitous moments?

FOR NEXT WEEK:

☐
☐
☐
☐
☐
☐
☐
☐
☐
☐
☐
☐
☐
☐

I am...

I don't go by the rule book....
I lead from the heart, not the head.

— DIANA, PRINCESS OF WALES

MONDAY	TUESDAY	WEDNESDAY

TODAY'S TOP 5:

☐
☐
☐
☐
☐

DWELL IN GRATITUDE:

♡
♡
♡

TODAY'S TOP 5:

☐
☐
☐
☐
☐

DWELL IN GRATITUDE:

♡
♡
♡

TODAY'S TOP 5:

☐
☐
☐
☐
☐

DWELL IN GRATITUDE:

♡
♡
♡

MASTERY & WELL-BEING:

H2O ⬜⬜⬜⬜⬜⬜⬜

EXERCISE 15 15 15 15 15 15 15

☐ DAILY HABIT

MASTERY & WELL-BEING:

H2O ⬜⬜⬜⬜⬜⬜⬜

EXERCISE 15 15 15 15 15 15 15

☐ DAILY HABIT

MASTERY & WELL-BEING:

H2O ⬜⬜⬜⬜⬜⬜⬜

EXERCISE 15 15 15 15 15 15 15

☐ DAILY HABIT

DELIVERABLES:

RECEIVABLES:

THURSDAY

TODAY'S TOP 5:

☐
☐
☐
☐
☐

DWELL IN GRATITUDE:

♡
♡
♡

MASTERY & WELL-BEING:

H2O 🥤🥤🥤🥤🥤🥤🥤

EXERCISE 🏃🏃🏃🏃🏃🏃🏃
15 15 15 15 15 15 15

☐ DAILY HABIT

FRIDAY

TODAY'S TOP 5:

☐
☐
☐
☐
☐

DWELL IN GRATITUDE:

♡
♡
♡

MASTERY & WELL-BEING:

H2O 🥤🥤🥤🥤🥤🥤🥤

EXERCISE 🏃🏃🏃🏃🏃🏃🏃
15 15 15 15 15 15 15

☐ DAILY HABIT

SATURDAY

SUNDAY

WEEKLY REFLECTION:

How are you feeling about the progress made towards your big picture milestones this week?

What are you most proud of this week?

Are you on track for conquering the big picture milestones you set for this sprint? Could you have done anything differently?

Did you stay on top of your health and maintain your new habit?

Did you have any big insights or serendipitous moments?

FOR NEXT WEEK:

☐
☐
☐
☐
☐
☐
☐
☐
☐
☐
☐
☐
☐
☐

I am...

*Do not wait on a leader ...
look in the mirror. it's you!*

– KATHERINE MIRACLE, MOTIVATIONAL SPEAKER

MONDAY	TUESDAY	WEDNESDAY
TODAY'S TOP 5:	TODAY'S TOP 5:	TODAY'S TOP 5:
☐	☐	☐
☐	☐	☐
☐	☐	☐
☐	☐	☐
☐	☐	☐
DWELL IN GRATITUDE:	DWELL IN GRATITUDE:	DWELL IN GRATITUDE:
♡	♡	♡
♡	♡	♡
♡	♡	♡

MASTERY & WELL-BEING:	MASTERY & WELL-BEING:	MASTERY & WELL-BEING:
H2O 🥛🥛🥛🥛🥛🥛🥛	H2O 🥛🥛🥛🥛🥛🥛🥛	H2O 🥛🥛🥛🥛🥛🥛🥛
EXERCISE 🏃🏃🏃🏃🏃🏃	EXERCISE 🏃🏃🏃🏃🏃🏃	EXERCISE 🏃🏃🏃🏃🏃🏃
15 15 15 15 15 15	15 15 15 15 15 15	15 15 15 15 15 15
☐ DAILY HABIT	☐ DAILY HABIT	☐ DAILY HABIT

DELIVERABLES:

RECEIVABLES:

THURSDAY

TODAY'S TOP 5:

☐
☐
☐
☐
☐

DWELL IN GRATITUDE:

♡
♡
♡

MASTERY & WELL-BEING:

H2O ▯ ▯ ▯ ▯ ▯ ▯ ▯

EXERCISE 🏃 🏃 🏃 🏃 🏃 🏃 🏃
      15 15 15 15 15 15 15

☐ DAILY HABIT

FRIDAY

TODAY'S TOP 5:

☐
☐
☐
☐
☐

DWELL IN GRATITUDE:

♡
♡
♡

MASTERY & WELL-BEING:

H2O ▯ ▯ ▯ ▯ ▯ ▯ ▯

EXERCISE 🏃 🏃 🏃 🏃 🏃 🏃 🏃
      15 15 15 15 15 15 15

☐ DAILY HABIT

SATURDAY

SUNDAY

WEEKLY REFLECTION:

How are you feeling about the progress made towards your big picture milestones this week?

😁 😍 😊 😐 😟 😫

What are you most proud of this week?

Are you on track for conquering the big picture milestones you set for this sprint? Could you have done anything differently?

Did you stay on top of your health and maintain your new habit?

Did you have any big insights or serendipitous moments?

FOR NEXT WEEK:

☐
☐
☐
☐
☐
☐
☐
☐
☐
☐
☐
☐
☐
☐

I am...

*Knowing what must be done
does away with fear.*

– ROSA PARKS, CIVIL RIGHTS ACTIVIST

MONDAY	TUESDAY	WEDNESDAY
TODAY'S TOP 5:	TODAY'S TOP 5:	TODAY'S TOP 5:
☐	☐	☐
☐	☐	☐
☐	☐	☐
☐	☐	☐
☐	☐	☐
DWELL IN GRATITUDE:	DWELL IN GRATITUDE:	DWELL IN GRATITUDE:
♡	♡	♡
♡	♡	♡
♡	♡	♡

MASTERY & WELL-BEING:	MASTERY & WELL-BEING:	MASTERY & WELL-BEING:
H2O ⊔ ⊔ ⊔ ⊔ ⊔ ⊔ ⊔	H2O ⊔ ⊔ ⊔ ⊔ ⊔ ⊔ ⊔	H2O ⊔ ⊔ ⊔ ⊔ ⊔ ⊔ ⊔
EXERCISE 🏃15 🏃15 🏃15 🏃15 🏃15 🏃15	EXERCISE 🏃15 🏃15 🏃15 🏃15 🏃15 🏃15	EXERCISE 🏃15 🏃15 🏃15 🏃15 🏃15 🏃15
☐ DAILY HABIT	☐ DAILY HABIT	☐ DAILY HABIT

DELIVERABLES:

RECEIVABLES:

BIG PICTURE PRIORITIES TO FOCUS ON:

DATE

THURSDAY

TODAY'S TOP 5:

- [ ]
- [ ]
- [ ]
- [ ]
- [ ]

DWELL IN GRATITUDE:

♡
♡
♡

MASTERY & WELL-BEING:

H2O 🥛🥛🥛🥛🥛🥛🥛

EXERCISE 🏃🏃🏃🏃🏃🏃🏃
15 15 15 15 15 15 15

- [ ] DAILY HABIT

FRIDAY

TODAY'S TOP 5:

- [ ]
- [ ]
- [ ]
- [ ]
- [ ]

DWELL IN GRATITUDE:

♡
♡
♡

MASTERY & WELL-BEING:

H2O 🥛🥛🥛🥛🥛🥛🥛

EXERCISE 🏃🏃🏃🏃🏃🏃🏃
15 15 15 15 15 15 15

- [ ] DAILY HABIT

SATURDAY

SUNDAY

WEEKLY REFLECTION:

How are you feeling about the progress made towards your big picture milestones this week?

What are you most proud of this week?

Are you on track for conquering the big picture milestones you set for this sprint? Could you have done anything differently?

Did you stay on top of your health and maintain your new habit?

Did you have any big insights or serendipitous moments?

FOR NEXT WEEK:

- [ ]
- [ ]
- [ ]
- [ ]
- [ ]
- [ ]
- [ ]
- [ ]
- [ ]
- [ ]
- [ ]
- [ ]
- [ ]

If we can learn to deal with our discomfort and just relax into it we'll have a better life.

– MELLODY HOBSON, BUSINESSWOMAN

MONDAY	TUESDAY	WEDNESDAY
TODAY'S TOP 5:	TODAY'S TOP 5:	TODAY'S TOP 5:
☐	☐	☐
☐	☐	☐
☐	☐	☐
☐	☐	☐
☐	☐	☐
DWELL IN GRATITUDE:	DWELL IN GRATITUDE:	DWELL IN GRATITUDE:
♡	♡	♡
♡	♡	♡
♡	♡	♡

MASTERY & WELL-BEING:	MASTERY & WELL-BEING:	MASTERY & WELL-BEING:
H2O ⬜⬜⬜⬜⬜⬜⬜⬜	H2O ⬜⬜⬜⬜⬜⬜⬜⬜	H2O ⬜⬜⬜⬜⬜⬜⬜⬜
EXERCISE 🚶🚶🚶🚶🚶🚶🚶 15 15 15 15 15 15 15	EXERCISE 🚶🚶🚶🚶🚶🚶🚶 15 15 15 15 15 15 15	EXERCISE 🚶🚶🚶🚶🚶🚶🚶 15 15 15 15 15 15 15
☐ DAILY HABIT	☐ DAILY HABIT	☐ DAILY HABIT

DELIVERABLES:

RECEIVABLES:

THURSDAY

TODAY'S TOP 5:

☐
☐
☐
☐
☐

DWELL IN GRATITUDE:

♡
♡
♡

MASTERY & WELL-BEING:

H2O ⊔ ⊔ ⊔ ⊔ ⊔ ⊔ ⊔

EXERCISE 🏃 🏃 🏃 🏃 🏃 🏃 🏃
15 15 15 15 15 15 15

☐ DAILY HABIT

FRIDAY

TODAY'S TOP 5:

☐
☐
☐
☐
☐

DWELL IN GRATITUDE:

♡
♡
♡

MASTERY & WELL-BEING:

H2O ⊔ ⊔ ⊔ ⊔ ⊔ ⊔ ⊔

EXERCISE 🏃 🏃 🏃 🏃 🏃 🏃 🏃
15 15 15 15 15 15 15

☐ DAILY HABIT

SATURDAY

SUNDAY

WEEKLY REFLECTION:

How are you feeling about the progress made towards your big picture milestones this week?

😁 😍 😊 😐 😟 😣

What are you most proud of this week?

Are you on track for conquering the big picture milestones you set for this sprint? Could you have done anything differently?

Did you stay on top of your health and maintain your new habit?

Did you have any big insights or serendipitous moments?

FOR NEXT WEEK:

☐
☐
☐
☐
☐
☐
☐
☐
☐
☐
☐
☐
☐
☐

I was smart enough to go through any door that opened.

– JOAN RIVERS, COMEDIAN AND ACTOR

MONDAY	TUESDAY	WEDNESDAY
TODAY'S TOP 5:	**TODAY'S TOP 5:**	**TODAY'S TOP 5:**
☐	☐	☐
☐	☐	☐
☐	☐	☐
☐	☐	☐
☐	☐	☐
DWELL IN GRATITUDE:	**DWELL IN GRATITUDE:**	**DWELL IN GRATITUDE:**
♡	♡	♡
♡	♡	♡
♡	♡	♡

MASTERY & WELL-BEING:	MASTERY & WELL-BEING:	MASTERY & WELL-BEING:
H2O ⬚⬚⬚⬚⬚⬚⬚	H2O ⬚⬚⬚⬚⬚⬚⬚	H2O ⬚⬚⬚⬚⬚⬚⬚
EXERCISE 🏃🏃🏃🏃🏃🏃🏃 15 15 15 15 15 15 15	EXERCISE 🏃🏃🏃🏃🏃🏃🏃 15 15 15 15 15 15 15	EXERCISE 🏃🏃🏃🏃🏃🏃🏃 15 15 15 15 15 15 15
☐ DAILY HABIT	☐ DAILY HABIT	☐ DAILY HABIT

DELIVERABLES:

RECEIVABLES:

THURSDAY

TODAY'S TOP 5:

☐
☐
☐
☐
☐

DWELL IN GRATITUDE:

♡
♡
♡

MASTERY & WELL-BEING:

H2O ☐ ☐ ☐ ☐ ☐ ☐ ☐

EXERCISE 🏃 🏃 🏃 🏃 🏃 🏃 🏃
15 15 15 15 15 15 15

☐ DAILY HABIT

FRIDAY

TODAY'S TOP 5:

☐
☐
☐
☐
☐

DWELL IN GRATITUDE:

♡
♡
♡

MASTERY & WELL-BEING:

H2O ☐ ☐ ☐ ☐ ☐ ☐ ☐

EXERCISE 🏃 🏃 🏃 🏃 🏃 🏃 🏃
15 15 15 15 15 15 15

☐ DAILY HABIT

SATURDAY

SUNDAY

WEEKLY REFLECTION:

How are you feeling about the progress made towards your big picture milestones this week?

😁 😍 😊 😐 😟 😣

What are you most proud of this week?

Are you on track for conquering the big picture milestones you set for this sprint? Could you have done anything differently?

Did you stay on top of your health and maintain your new habit?

Did you have any big insights or serendipitous moments?

FOR NEXT WEEK:

☐
☐
☐
☐
☐
☐
☐
☐
☐
☐
☐
☐
☐

The difference between successful people and others is how long they spend time feeling sorry for themselves.

– BARBARA CORCORAN, BUSINESSWOMAN

MONDAY	TUESDAY	WEDNESDAY

TODAY'S TOP 5:

☐
☐
☐
☐
☐

DWELL IN GRATITUDE:

♡
♡
♡

MASTERY & WELL-BEING:

H2O ⊔ ⊔ ⊔ ⊔ ⊔ ⊔ ⊔

EXERCISE 🏃 🏃 🏃 🏃 🏃 🏃 🏃
15 15 15 15 15 15 15

☐ DAILY HABIT

TODAY'S TOP 5:

☐
☐
☐
☐
☐

DWELL IN GRATITUDE:

♡
♡
♡

MASTERY & WELL-BEING:

H2O ⊔ ⊔ ⊔ ⊔ ⊔ ⊔ ⊔

EXERCISE 🏃 🏃 🏃 🏃 🏃 🏃 🏃
15 15 15 15 15 15 15

☐ DAILY HABIT

TODAY'S TOP 5:

☐
☐
☐
☐
☐

DWELL IN GRATITUDE:

♡
♡
♡

MASTERY & WELL-BEING:

H2O ⊔ ⊔ ⊔ ⊔ ⊔ ⊔ ⊔

EXERCISE 🏃 🏃 🏃 🏃 🏃 🏃 🏃
15 15 15 15 15 15 15

☐ DAILY HABIT

DELIVERABLES:

RECEIVABLES:

BIG PICTURE PRIORITIES TO FOCUS ON:

DATE

THURSDAY

TODAY'S TOP 5:

- [ ]
- [ ]
- [ ]
- [ ]
- [ ]

DWELL IN GRATITUDE:

- ♡
- ♡
- ♡

MASTERY & WELL-BEING:

H2O 🥛🥛🥛🥛🥛🥛🥛

EXERCISE 🏃🏃🏃🏃🏃🏃🏃
         15 15 15 15 15 15 15

- [ ] DAILY HABIT

FRIDAY

TODAY'S TOP 5:

- [ ]
- [ ]
- [ ]
- [ ]
- [ ]

DWELL IN GRATITUDE:

- ♡
- ♡
- ♡

MASTERY & WELL-BEING:

H2O 🥛🥛🥛🥛🥛🥛🥛

EXERCISE 🏃🏃🏃🏃🏃🏃🏃
         15 15 15 15 15 15 15

- [ ] DAILY HABIT

SATURDAY

SUNDAY

WEEKLY REFLECTION:

How are you feeling about the progress made towards your big picture milestones this week?

What are you most proud of this week?

Are you on track for conquering the big picture milestones you set for this sprint? Could you have done anything differently?

Did you stay on top of your health and maintain your new habit?

Did you have any big insights or serendipitous moments?

FOR NEXT WEEK:

- [ ]
- [ ]
- [ ]
- [ ]
- [ ]
- [ ]
- [ ]
- [ ]
- [ ]
- [ ]
- [ ]
- [ ]
- [ ]

I am...

Don't compromise yourself. You're all you've got.

– JANIS JOPLIN, SINGER-SONGWRITER

MONDAY	TUESDAY	WEDNESDAY

TODAY'S TOP 5:

☐
☐
☐
☐
☐

DWELL IN GRATITUDE:

♡
♡
♡

TODAY'S TOP 5:

☐
☐
☐
☐
☐

DWELL IN GRATITUDE:

♡
♡
♡

TODAY'S TOP 5:

☐
☐
☐
☐
☐

DWELL IN GRATITUDE:

♡
♡
♡

MASTERY & WELL-BEING:

H2O ▢ ▢ ▢ ▢ ▢ ▢ ▢

EXERCISE 🏃 🏃 🏃 🏃 🏃 🏃 🏃
15 15 15 15 15 15 15

☐ DAILY HABIT

MASTERY & WELL-BEING:

H2O ▢ ▢ ▢ ▢ ▢ ▢ ▢

EXERCISE 🏃 🏃 🏃 🏃 🏃 🏃 🏃
15 15 15 15 15 15 15

☐ DAILY HABIT

MASTERY & WELL-BEING:

H2O ▢ ▢ ▢ ▢ ▢ ▢ ▢

EXERCISE 🏃 🏃 🏃 🏃 🏃 🏃 🏃
15 15 15 15 15 15 15

☐ DAILY HABIT

DELIVERABLES:

RECEIVABLES:

BIG PICTURE PRIORITIES TO FOCUS ON:

DATE

THURSDAY	FRIDAY	SATURDAY

TODAY'S TOP 5:
- ☐
- ☐
- ☐
- ☐
- ☐

TODAY'S TOP 5:
- ☐
- ☐
- ☐
- ☐
- ☐

DWELL IN GRATITUDE:
- ♡
- ♡
- ♡

DWELL IN GRATITUDE:
- ♡
- ♡
- ♡

SUNDAY

MASTERY & WELL-BEING:

H2O ⊔ ⊔ ⊔ ⊔ ⊔ ⊔ ⊔ ⊔

EXERCISE 🏃 🏃 🏃 🏃 🏃 🏃 🏃
15 15 15 15 15 15 15

☐ DAILY HABIT

MASTERY & WELL-BEING:

H2O ⊔ ⊔ ⊔ ⊔ ⊔ ⊔ ⊔ ⊔

EXERCISE 🏃 🏃 🏃 🏃 🏃 🏃 🏃
15 15 15 15 15 15 15

☐ DAILY HABIT

WEEKLY REFLECTION:

How are you feeling about the progress made towards your big picture milestones this week?

😁 😍 🙂 😐 🙁 ☹️

What are you most proud of this week?

Are you on track for conquering the big picture milestones you set for this sprint? Could you have done anything differently?

Did you stay on top of your health and maintain your new habit?

Did you have any big insights or serendipitous moments?

FOR NEXT WEEK:

- ☐
- ☐
- ☐
- ☐
- ☐
- ☐
- ☐
- ☐
- ☐
- ☐
- ☐
- ☐
- ☐
- ☐

I am...

You must learn to be still in the midst of activity and to be vibrantly alive in repose.

– INDIRA GANDHI, STATESWOMAN

MONDAY	TUESDAY	WEDNESDAY

TODAY'S TOP 5:

☐
☐
☐
☐
☐

DWELL IN GRATITUDE:

♡
♡
♡

TODAY'S TOP 5:

☐
☐
☐
☐
☐

DWELL IN GRATITUDE:

♡
♡
♡

TODAY'S TOP 5:

☐
☐
☐
☐
☐

DWELL IN GRATITUDE:

♡
♡
♡

MASTERY & WELL-BEING:

H2O ⬜⬜⬜⬜⬜⬜⬜⬜

EXERCISE 🏃🏃🏃🏃🏃🏃🏃
15 15 15 15 15 15

☐ DAILY HABIT

MASTERY & WELL-BEING:

H2O ⬜⬜⬜⬜⬜⬜⬜⬜

EXERCISE 🏃🏃🏃🏃🏃🏃🏃
15 15 15 15 15 15

☐ DAILY HABIT

MASTERY & WELL-BEING:

H2O ⬜⬜⬜⬜⬜⬜⬜⬜

EXERCISE 🏃🏃🏃🏃🏃🏃🏃
15 15 15 15 15 15

☐ DAILY HABIT

DELIVERABLES:

RECEIVABLES:

_____

DATE

THURSDAY

TODAY'S TOP 5:

☐
☐
☐
☐
☐

DWELL IN GRATITUDE:

♡
♡
♡

MASTERY & WELL-BEING:

H2O ⊔ ⊔ ⊔ ⊔ ⊔ ⊔ ⊔

EXERCISE 🏃 🏃 🏃 🏃 🏃 🏃 🏃
       15 15 15 15 15 15 15

☐ DAILY HABIT

FRIDAY

TODAY'S TOP 5:

☐
☐
☐
☐
☐

DWELL IN GRATITUDE:

♡
♡
♡

MASTERY & WELL-BEING:

H2O ⊔ ⊔ ⊔ ⊔ ⊔ ⊔ ⊔

EXERCISE 🏃 🏃 🏃 🏃 🏃 🏃 🏃
       15 15 15 15 15 15 15

☐ DAILY HABIT

SATURDAY

SUNDAY

WEEKLY REFLECTION:

How are you feeling about the progress made towards your big picture milestones this week?

😁 😍 🙂 😐 😟 ☹️

What are you most proud of this week?

Are you on track for conquering the big picture milestones you set for this sprint? Could you have done anything differently?

Did you stay on top of your health and maintain your new habit?

Did you have any big insights or serendipitous moments?

FOR NEXT WEEK:

☐
☐
☐
☐
☐
☐
☐
☐
☐
☐
☐
☐
☐
☐

I love to see a young girl go out and grab the world by the lapels. Life's a bitch. You've got to go out and kick ass.

— MAYA ANGELOU, POET

MONDAY	TUESDAY	WEDNESDAY
TODAY'S TOP 5:	**TODAY'S TOP 5:**	**TODAY'S TOP 5:**
☐	☐	☐
☐	☐	☐
☐	☐	☐
☐	☐	☐
☐	☐	☐
DWELL IN GRATITUDE:	**DWELL IN GRATITUDE:**	**DWELL IN GRATITUDE:**
♡	♡	♡
♡	♡	♡
♡	♡	♡

MASTERY & WELL-BEING:

MONDAY
H2O 🥛🥛🥛🥛🥛🥛🥛🥛
EXERCISE 🏃15 🏃15 🏃15 🏃15 🏃15 🏃15
☐ DAILY HABIT

TUESDAY
H2O 🥛🥛🥛🥛🥛🥛🥛🥛
EXERCISE 🏃15 🏃15 🏃15 🏃15 🏃15 🏃15
☐ DAILY HABIT

WEDNESDAY
H2O 🥛🥛🥛🥛🥛🥛🥛🥛
EXERCISE 🏃15 🏃15 🏃15 🏃15 🏃15 🏃15
☐ DAILY HABIT

DELIVERABLES:

RECEIVABLES:

THURSDAY

TODAY'S TOP 5:

- [ ]
- [ ]
- [ ]
- [ ]
- [ ]

DWELL IN GRATITUDE:

♡
♡
♡

MASTERY & WELL-BEING:

H2O ⊔ ⊔ ⊔ ⊔ ⊔ ⊔ ⊔

EXERCISE 🚶 🚶 🚶 🚶 🚶 🚶 🚶
15 15 15 15 15 15 15

- [ ] DAILY HABIT

FRIDAY

TODAY'S TOP 5:

- [ ]
- [ ]
- [ ]
- [ ]
- [ ]

DWELL IN GRATITUDE:

♡
♡
♡

MASTERY & WELL-BEING:

H2O ⊔ ⊔ ⊔ ⊔ ⊔ ⊔ ⊔

EXERCISE 🚶 🚶 🚶 🚶 🚶 🚶 🚶
15 15 15 15 15 15 15

- [ ] DAILY HABIT

SATURDAY

SUNDAY

WEEKLY REFLECTION:

How are you feeling about the progress made towards your big picture milestones this week?

What are you most proud of this week?

Are you on track for conquering the big picture milestones you set for this sprint? Could you have done anything differently?

Did you stay on top of your health and maintain your new habit?

Did you have any big insights or serendipitous moments?

FOR NEXT WEEK:

- [ ]
- [ ]
- [ ]
- [ ]
- [ ]
- [ ]
- [ ]
- [ ]
- [ ]
- [ ]
- [ ]
- [ ]
- [ ]
- [ ]

Great work! I hope you're fired up and feeling ready for the final sprint of the year ahead.

What are you most proud of achieving in the last twelve weeks?

Did you accomplish your "Balanced Ambition" goals and desires?

What milestones did you conquer for your Big Picture Goals? Which ones need to be pushed back or adjusted?

How did you reward yourself for all you achieved the last twelve weeks?

How are you feeling about the new habit you cemented into your daily routine?

How do you feel about the last quarter overall?

SPRINT 4

Sprint: _____

You are worthy of every wish, dream, goal, and desire in your heart for the year ahead.

BIG PICTURE MILESTONES

1. ....
2. ....
3. ....
4. ....
5. ....
6. ....
7. ....

BRAIN DUMP

List every task you can think of for each milestone above.

☐ PUT THESE INTO A PROJECT MANAGEMENT SYSTEM AND ASSIGN DEADLINES

Don't be shy about your passion, your love, your success. Stand up and shout your truth—the world needs to hear it.

- NATALIE MACNEIL

BALANCED AMBITION

HABIT:	LEARNING:	GIVING BACK:

HEALTH:	RELATIONSHIPS:	ADVENTURE:

CONSCIOUS CREATION

What are you creating to share your talents and gifts with the world?

BLOG POST, VIDEO OR SOCIAL MEDIA CONTENT I WANT TO CREATE	OUTLINE	DRAFT	EDIT	PUBLISH

VISUALIZATION

What will your life look like and feel like if you conquer these goals and milestones?

SPRINT REWARD

How will you reward yourself for achieving these milestones and goals?

I am...

When we do the best we can, we never know what miracle is wrought in our life, or in the life of another.

— HELEN KELLER, AUTHOR

MONDAY	TUESDAY	WEDNESDAY
TODAY'S TOP 5:	TODAY'S TOP 5:	TODAY'S TOP 5:
☐	☐	☐
☐	☐	☐
☐	☐	☐
☐	☐	☐
☐	☐	☐
DWELL IN GRATITUDE:	DWELL IN GRATITUDE:	DWELL IN GRATITUDE:
♡	♡	♡
♡	♡	♡
♡	♡	♡
MASTERY & WELL-BEING:	MASTERY & WELL-BEING:	MASTERY & WELL-BEING:
H2O ⬜⬜⬜⬜⬜⬜⬜⬜	H2O ⬜⬜⬜⬜⬜⬜⬜⬜	H2O ⬜⬜⬜⬜⬜⬜⬜⬜
EXERCISE 15 15 15 15 15 15 15	EXERCISE 15 15 15 15 15 15 15	EXERCISE 15 15 15 15 15 15 15
☐ DAILY HABIT	☐ DAILY HABIT	☐ DAILY HABIT

DELIVERABLES:

RECEIVABLES:

THURSDAY

TODAY'S TOP 5:

- [ ]
- [ ]
- [ ]
- [ ]
- [ ]

DWELL IN GRATITUDE:

♡
♡
♡

MASTERY & WELL-BEING:

H2O 🥛🥛🥛🥛🥛🥛🥛

EXERCISE 🏃🏃🏃🏃🏃🏃🏃
15 15 15 15 15 15 15

- [ ] DAILY HABIT

FRIDAY

TODAY'S TOP 5:

- [ ]
- [ ]
- [ ]
- [ ]
- [ ]

DWELL IN GRATITUDE:

♡
♡
♡

MASTERY & WELL-BEING:

H2O 🥛🥛🥛🥛🥛🥛🥛

EXERCISE 🏃🏃🏃🏃🏃🏃🏃
15 15 15 15 15 15 15

- [ ] DAILY HABIT

SATURDAY

SUNDAY

WEEKLY REFLECTION:

How are you feeling about the progress made towards your big picture milestones this week?

What are you most proud of this week?

Are you on track for conquering the big picture milestones you set for this sprint? Could you have done anything differently?

Did you stay on top of your health and maintain your new habit?

Did you have any big insights or serendipitous moments?

FOR NEXT WEEK:

- [ ]
- [ ]
- [ ]
- [ ]
- [ ]
- [ ]
- [ ]
- [ ]
- [ ]
- [ ]
- [ ]
- [ ]
- [ ]
- [ ]

If you obey all the rules, you miss all the fun.

– KATHARINE HEPBURN, ACTRESS

MONDAY	TUESDAY	WEDNESDAY

TODAY'S TOP 5:

☐
☐
☐
☐
☐

DWELL IN GRATITUDE:

♡
♡
♡

TODAY'S TOP 5:

☐
☐
☐
☐
☐

DWELL IN GRATITUDE:

♡
♡
♡

TODAY'S TOP 5:

☐
☐
☐
☐
☐

DWELL IN GRATITUDE:

♡
♡
♡

MASTERY & WELL-BEING:

H2O 🥛🥛🥛🥛🥛🥛🥛🥛

EXERCISE 🏃🏃🏃🏃🏃🏃🏃
15 15 15 15 15 15

☐ DAILY HABIT

MASTERY & WELL-BEING:

H2O 🥛🥛🥛🥛🥛🥛🥛🥛

EXERCISE 🏃🏃🏃🏃🏃🏃🏃
15 15 15 15 15 15

☐ DAILY HABIT

MASTERY & WELL-BEING:

H2O 🥛🥛🥛🥛🥛🥛🥛🥛

EXERCISE 🏃🏃🏃🏃🏃🏃🏃
15 15 15 15 15 15

☐ DAILY HABIT

DELIVERABLES:

RECEIVABLES:

BIG PICTURE PRIORITIES TO FOCUS ON:

DATE

THURSDAY

TODAY'S TOP 5:
- ☐
- ☐
- ☐
- ☐
- ☐

DWELL IN GRATITUDE:
- ♡
- ♡
- ♡

MASTERY & WELL-BEING:

H2O ▯ ▯ ▯ ▯ ▯ ▯ ▯

EXERCISE 🏃 🏃 🏃 🏃 🏃 🏃
15   15   15   15   15   15

☐ DAILY HABIT

FRIDAY

TODAY'S TOP 5:
- ☐
- ☐
- ☐
- ☐
- ☐

DWELL IN GRATITUDE:
- ♡
- ♡
- ♡

MASTERY & WELL-BEING:

H2O ▯ ▯ ▯ ▯ ▯ ▯ ▯

EXERCISE 🏃 🏃 🏃 🏃 🏃 🏃
15   15   15   15   15   15

☐ DAILY HABIT

SATURDAY

SUNDAY

WEEKLY REFLECTION:

How are you feeling about the progress made towards your big picture milestones this week?

😁 😍 😃 😐 😟 😣

What are you most proud of this week?

Are you on track for conquering the big picture milestones you set for this sprint? Could you have done anything differently?

Did you stay on top of your health and maintain your new habit?

Did you have any big insights or serendipitous moments?

FOR NEXT WEEK:
- ☐
- ☐
- ☐
- ☐
- ☐
- ☐
- ☐
- ☐
- ☐
- ☐
- ☐
- ☐
- ☐
- ☐

I am...

Life shrinks or expands in proportion to one's courage.

– ANAÏS NIN, ESSAYIST

MONDAY	TUESDAY	WEDNESDAY
TODAY'S TOP 5:	**TODAY'S TOP 5:**	**TODAY'S TOP 5:**
☐	☐	☐
☐	☐	☐
☐	☐	☐
☐	☐	☐
☐	☐	☐
DWELL IN GRATITUDE:	**DWELL IN GRATITUDE:**	**DWELL IN GRATITUDE:**
♡	♡	♡
♡	♡	♡
♡	♡	♡

MASTERY & WELL-BEING:	MASTERY & WELL-BEING:	MASTERY & WELL-BEING:
H2O ⬚⬚⬚⬚⬚⬚⬚	H2O ⬚⬚⬚⬚⬚⬚⬚	H2O ⬚⬚⬚⬚⬚⬚⬚
EXERCISE (15 15 15 15 15 15)	EXERCISE (15 15 15 15 15 15)	EXERCISE (15 15 15 15 15 15)
☐ DAILY HABIT	☐ DAILY HABIT	☐ DAILY HABIT

DELIVERABLES:

RECEIVABLES:

THURSDAY

TODAY'S TOP 5:

- ☐
- ☐
- ☐
- ☐
- ☐

DWELL IN GRATITUDE:

- ♡
- ♡
- ♡

MASTERY & WELL-BEING:

H2O 🥛🥛🥛🥛🥛🥛🥛🥛

EXERCISE 🏃🏃🏃🏃🏃🏃🏃
15 15 15 15 15 15 15

☐ DAILY HABIT

FRIDAY

TODAY'S TOP 5:

- ☐
- ☐
- ☐
- ☐
- ☐

DWELL IN GRATITUDE:

- ♡
- ♡
- ♡

MASTERY & WELL-BEING:

H2O 🥛🥛🥛🥛🥛🥛🥛🥛

EXERCISE 🏃🏃🏃🏃🏃🏃🏃
15 15 15 15 15 15 15

☐ DAILY HABIT

SATURDAY

SUNDAY

WEEKLY REFLECTION:

How are you feeling about the progress made towards your big picture milestones this week?

😁 😍 🙂 😐 🙁 ☹️

What are you most proud of this week?

Are you on track for conquering the big picture milestones you set for this sprint? Could you have done anything differently?

Did you stay on top of your health and maintain your new habit?

Did you have any big insights or serendipitous moments?

FOR NEXT WEEK:

- ☐
- ☐
- ☐
- ☐
- ☐
- ☐
- ☐
- ☐
- ☐
- ☐
- ☐
- ☐
- ☐
- ☐

Never give up, for that is just the place and time that the tide will turn.

– HARRIET BEECHER STOWE, AUTHOR

MONDAY	TUESDAY	WEDNESDAY
TODAY'S TOP 5:	**TODAY'S TOP 5:**	**TODAY'S TOP 5:**
☐	☐	☐
☐	☐	☐
☐	☐	☐
☐	☐	☐
☐	☐	☐
DWELL IN GRATITUDE:	**DWELL IN GRATITUDE:**	**DWELL IN GRATITUDE:**
♡	♡	♡
♡	♡	♡
♡	♡	♡

MASTERY & WELL-BEING:

MONDAY
H2O ▯▯▯▯▯▯▯▯
EXERCISE 15 15 15 15 15 15 15
☐ DAILY HABIT

TUESDAY
H2O ▯▯▯▯▯▯▯▯
EXERCISE 15 15 15 15 15 15 15
☐ DAILY HABIT

WEDNESDAY
H2O ▯▯▯▯▯▯▯▯
EXERCISE 15 15 15 15 15 15 15
☐ DAILY HABIT

DELIVERABLES:

RECEIVABLES:

THURSDAY

TODAY'S TOP 5:

- [ ]
- [ ]
- [ ]
- [ ]
- [ ]

DWELL IN GRATITUDE:

♡
♡
♡

MASTERY & WELL-BEING:

H2O 🥛🥛🥛🥛🥛🥛🥛

EXERCISE 🏃🏃🏃🏃🏃🏃🏃
15 15 15 15 15 15 15

- [ ] DAILY HABIT

FRIDAY

TODAY'S TOP 5:

- [ ]
- [ ]
- [ ]
- [ ]
- [ ]

DWELL IN GRATITUDE:

♡
♡
♡

MASTERY & WELL-BEING:

H2O 🥛🥛🥛🥛🥛🥛🥛

EXERCISE 🏃🏃🏃🏃🏃🏃🏃
15 15 15 15 15 15 15

- [ ] DAILY HABIT

SATURDAY

SUNDAY

WEEKLY REFLECTION:

How are you feeling about the progress made towards your big picture milestones this week?

😁 😍 😃 😐 ☹️ 😣

What are you most proud of this week?

Are you on track for conquering the big picture milestones you set for this sprint? Could you have done anything differently?

Did you stay on top of your health and maintain your new habit?

Did you have any big insights or serendipitous moments?

FOR NEXT WEEK:

- [ ]
- [ ]
- [ ]
- [ ]
- [ ]
- [ ]
- [ ]
- [ ]
- [ ]
- [ ]
- [ ]
- [ ]
- [ ]
- [ ]

A lot of people are afraid to say what they want. That's why they don't get what they want.

– MADONNA, SINGER-SONGWRITER

MONDAY	TUESDAY	WEDNESDAY
TODAY'S TOP 5:	TODAY'S TOP 5:	TODAY'S TOP 5:
☐	☐	☐
☐	☐	☐
☐	☐	☐
☐	☐	☐
☐	☐	☐
DWELL IN GRATITUDE:	DWELL IN GRATITUDE:	DWELL IN GRATITUDE:
♡	♡	♡
♡	♡	♡
♡	♡	♡

MASTERY & WELL-BEING:

	MONDAY	TUESDAY	WEDNESDAY
H2O	☐☐☐☐☐☐☐☐	☐☐☐☐☐☐☐☐	☐☐☐☐☐☐☐☐
EXERCISE	15 15 15 15 15 15 15	15 15 15 15 15 15 15	15 15 15 15 15 15 15
☐ DAILY HABIT	☐ DAILY HABIT	☐ DAILY HABIT

DELIVERABLES:

RECEIVABLES:

THURSDAY

TODAY'S TOP 5:

☐
☐
☐
☐
☐

DWELL IN GRATITUDE:

♡
♡
♡

MASTERY & WELL-BEING:

H2O ⊔⊔⊔⊔⊔⊔⊔

EXERCISE 🏃15 🏃15 🏃15 🏃15 🏃15 🏃15 🏃15

☐ DAILY HABIT

FRIDAY

TODAY'S TOP 5:

☐
☐
☐
☐
☐

DWELL IN GRATITUDE:

♡
♡
♡

MASTERY & WELL-BEING:

H2O ⊔⊔⊔⊔⊔⊔⊔

EXERCISE 🏃15 🏃15 🏃15 🏃15 🏃15 🏃15 🏃15

☐ DAILY HABIT

SATURDAY

SUNDAY

WEEKLY REFLECTION:

How are you feeling about the progress made towards your big picture milestones this week?

😁$$ 😍 🙂 😐 🙁 😞

What are you most proud of this week?

Are you on track for conquering the big picture milestones you set for this sprint? Could you have done anything differently?

Did you stay on top of your health and maintain your new habit?

Did you have any big insights or serendipitous moments?

FOR NEXT WEEK:

☐
☐
☐
☐
☐
☐
☐
☐
☐
☐
☐
☐
☐

I am...

Destiny is a name often given in retrospect to choices that had dramatic consequences.

– J. K. ROWLING, AUTHOR

MONDAY	TUESDAY	WEDNESDAY

TODAY'S TOP 5:

☐
☐
☐
☐
☐

DWELL IN GRATITUDE:

♡
♡
♡

TODAY'S TOP 5:

☐
☐
☐
☐
☐

DWELL IN GRATITUDE:

♡
♡
♡

TODAY'S TOP 5:

☐
☐
☐
☐
☐

DWELL IN GRATITUDE:

♡
♡
♡

MASTERY & WELL-BEING:

H2O ▯ ▯ ▯ ▯ ▯ ▯ ▯

EXERCISE 🏃 🏃 🏃 🏃 🏃 🏃 🏃
15 15 15 15 15 15 15

☐ DAILY HABIT

MASTERY & WELL-BEING:

H2O ▯ ▯ ▯ ▯ ▯ ▯ ▯

EXERCISE 🏃 🏃 🏃 🏃 🏃 🏃 🏃
15 15 15 15 15 15 15

☐ DAILY HABIT

MASTERY & WELL-BEING:

H2O ▯ ▯ ▯ ▯ ▯ ▯ ▯

EXERCISE 🏃 🏃 🏃 🏃 🏃 🏃 🏃
15 15 15 15 15 15 15

☐ DAILY HABIT

DELIVERABLES:

RECEIVABLES:

THURSDAY

TODAY'S TOP 5:

☐
☐
☐
☐
☐

DWELL IN GRATITUDE:

♡
♡
♡

MASTERY & WELL-BEING:

H2O ▯ ▯ ▯ ▯ ▯ ▯ ▯

EXERCISE 🏃 🏃 🏃 🏃 🏃 🏃 🏃
15 15 15 15 15 15 15

☐ DAILY HABIT

FRIDAY

TODAY'S TOP 5:

☐
☐
☐
☐
☐

DWELL IN GRATITUDE:

♡
♡
♡

MASTERY & WELL-BEING:

H2O ▯ ▯ ▯ ▯ ▯ ▯ ▯

EXERCISE 🏃 🏃 🏃 🏃 🏃 🏃 🏃
15 15 15 15 15 15 15

☐ DAILY HABIT

SATURDAY

SUNDAY

WEEKLY REFLECTION:

How are you feeling about the progress made towards your big picture milestones this week?

😁 😍 🙂 😐 😟 😣

What are you most proud of this week?

Are you on track for conquering the big picture milestones you set for this sprint? Could you have done anything differently?

Did you stay on top of your health and maintain your new habit?

Did you have any big insights or serendipitous moments?

FOR NEXT WEEK:

☐
☐
☐
☐
☐
☐
☐
☐
☐
☐
☐
☐
☐
☐

I am...

Stop wearing your wishbone where your backbone ought to be.

– ELIZABETH GILBERT, AUTHOR

MONDAY	TUESDAY	WEDNESDAY
TODAY'S TOP 5:	**TODAY'S TOP 5:**	**TODAY'S TOP 5:**
☐	☐	☐
☐	☐	☐
☐	☐	☐
☐	☐	☐
☐	☐	☐
DWELL IN GRATITUDE:	**DWELL IN GRATITUDE:**	**DWELL IN GRATITUDE:**
♡	♡	♡
♡	♡	♡
♡	♡	♡

MASTERY & WELL-BEING:	MASTERY & WELL-BEING:	MASTERY & WELL-BEING:
H2O ⊔⊔⊔⊔⊔⊔⊔⊔	H2O ⊔⊔⊔⊔⊔⊔⊔⊔	H2O ⊔⊔⊔⊔⊔⊔⊔⊔
EXERCISE 🏃🏃🏃🏃🏃🏃	EXERCISE 🏃🏃🏃🏃🏃🏃	EXERCISE 🏃🏃🏃🏃🏃🏃
15 15 15 15 15 15	15 15 15 15 15 15	15 15 15 15 15 15
☐ DAILY HABIT	☐ DAILY HABIT	☐ DAILY HABIT

DELIVERABLES:

RECEIVABLES:

BIG PICTURE PRIORITIES TO FOCUS ON:

THURSDAY	FRIDAY	SATURDAY

TODAY'S TOP 5:
- ☐
- ☐
- ☐
- ☐
- ☐

TODAY'S TOP 5:
- ☐
- ☐
- ☐
- ☐
- ☐

DWELL IN GRATITUDE:
- ♡
- ♡
- ♡

DWELL IN GRATITUDE:
- ♡
- ♡
- ♡

SUNDAY

MASTERY & WELL-BEING:

H2O ▯ ▯ ▯ ▯ ▯ ▯ ▯

EXERCISE 🏃 🏃 🏃 🏃 🏃 🏃 🏃
15   15   15   15   15   15   15

☐ DAILY HABIT

MASTERY & WELL-BEING:

H2O ▯ ▯ ▯ ▯ ▯ ▯ ▯

EXERCISE 🏃 🏃 🏃 🏃 🏃 🏃 🏃
15   15   15   15   15   15   15

☐ DAILY HABIT

WEEKLY REFLECTION:

How are you feeling about the progress made towards your big picture milestones this week?

😁($$) 😍 😀 😐 🙁 😣

What are you most proud of this week?

Are you on track for conquering the big picture milestones you set for this sprint? Could you have done anything differently?

Did you stay on top of your health and maintain your new habit?

Did you have any big insights or serendipitous moments?

FOR NEXT WEEK:

- ☐
- ☐
- ☐
- ☐
- ☐
- ☐
- ☐
- ☐
- ☐
- ☐
- ☐
- ☐
- ☐
- ☐

Just watch.... I'll show you what a woman can do....
I'll go across the country. I'll race to the Moon....
I'll never look back.

– EDNA GARDNER WHYTE, AVIATOR

MONDAY	TUESDAY	WEDNESDAY

TODAY'S TOP 5:

☐
☐
☐
☐
☐

DWELL IN GRATITUDE:

♡
♡
♡

TODAY'S TOP 5:

☐
☐
☐
☐
☐

DWELL IN GRATITUDE:

♡
♡
♡

TODAY'S TOP 5:

☐
☐
☐
☐
☐

DWELL IN GRATITUDE:

♡
♡
♡

MASTERY & WELL-BEING:

H2O ⊔⊔⊔⊔⊔⊔⊔⊔

EXERCISE 🏃🏃🏃🏃🏃🏃🏃
15 15 15 15 15 15 15

☐ DAILY HABIT

MASTERY & WELL-BEING:

H2O ⊔⊔⊔⊔⊔⊔⊔⊔

EXERCISE 🏃🏃🏃🏃🏃🏃🏃
15 15 15 15 15 15 15

☐ DAILY HABIT

MASTERY & WELL-BEING:

H2O ⊔⊔⊔⊔⊔⊔⊔⊔

EXERCISE 🏃🏃🏃🏃🏃🏃🏃
15 15 15 15 15 15 15

☐ DAILY HABIT

DELIVERABLES:

RECEIVABLES:

BIG PICTURE PRIORITIES TO FOCUS ON:

THURSDAY	FRIDAY	SATURDAY

THURSDAY

TODAY'S TOP 5:
- ☐
- ☐
- ☐
- ☐
- ☐

DWELL IN GRATITUDE:
- ♡
- ♡
- ♡

MASTERY & WELL-BEING:

H2O ⬚ ⬚ ⬚ ⬚ ⬚ ⬚ ⬚

EXERCISE 🏃 🏃 🏃 🏃 🏃 🏃 🏃
15 15 15 15 15 15 15

☐ DAILY HABIT

FRIDAY

TODAY'S TOP 5:
- ☐
- ☐
- ☐
- ☐
- ☐

DWELL IN GRATITUDE:
- ♡
- ♡
- ♡

MASTERY & WELL-BEING:

H2O ⬚ ⬚ ⬚ ⬚ ⬚ ⬚ ⬚

EXERCISE 🏃 🏃 🏃 🏃 🏃 🏃 🏃
15 15 15 15 15 15 15

☐ DAILY HABIT

SATURDAY

SUNDAY

WEEKLY REFLECTION:

How are you feeling about the progress made towards your big picture milestones this week?

😁 😍 😊 😐 😟 😫

What are you most proud of this week?

Are you on track for conquering the big picture milestones you set for this sprint? Could you have done anything differently?

Did you stay on top of your health and maintain your new habit?

Did you have any big insights or serendipitous moments?

FOR NEXT WEEK:

- ☐
- ☐
- ☐
- ☐
- ☐
- ☐
- ☐
- ☐
- ☐
- ☐
- ☐
- ☐
- ☐
- ☐

We must believe that we are gifted for something, and that this thing, at whatever cost, must be attained.

– MARIE CURIE, PHYSICIST AND CHEMIST

MONDAY	TUESDAY	WEDNESDAY
TODAY'S TOP 5:	TODAY'S TOP 5:	TODAY'S TOP 5:
☐	☐	☐
☐	☐	☐
☐	☐	☐
☐	☐	☐
☐	☐	☐
DWELL IN GRATITUDE:	DWELL IN GRATITUDE:	DWELL IN GRATITUDE:
♡	♡	♡
♡	♡	♡
♡	♡	♡

MASTERY & WELL-BEING:	MASTERY & WELL-BEING:	MASTERY & WELL-BEING:
H2O ⊽⊽⊽⊽⊽⊽⊽⊽	H2O ⊽⊽⊽⊽⊽⊽⊽⊽	H2O ⊽⊽⊽⊽⊽⊽⊽⊽
EXERCISE 15 15 15 15 15 15 15	EXERCISE 15 15 15 15 15 15 15	EXERCISE 15 15 15 15 15 15
☐ DAILY HABIT	☐ DAILY HABIT	☐ DAILY HABIT

DELIVERABLES:

RECEIVABLES:

THURSDAY	FRIDAY	SATURDAY
TODAY'S TOP 5:	**TODAY'S TOP 5:**	
☐	☐	
☐	☐	
☐	☐	
☐	☐	
☐	☐	

DWELL IN GRATITUDE: ♡ ♡ ♡

DWELL IN GRATITUDE: ♡ ♡ ♡

SUNDAY

MASTERY & WELL-BEING:

H2O ⊔ ⊔ ⊔ ⊔ ⊔ ⊔ ⊔

EXERCISE 🏃 🏃 🏃 🏃 🏃 🏃
15 15 15 15 15 15

☐ DAILY HABIT

MASTERY & WELL-BEING:

H2O ⊔ ⊔ ⊔ ⊔ ⊔ ⊔ ⊔

EXERCISE 🏃 🏃 🏃 🏃 🏃 🏃
15 15 15 15 15 15

☐ DAILY HABIT

WEEKLY REFLECTION:

How are you feeling about the progress made towards your big picture milestones this week?

😁 😍 😊 😐 😟 ☹️

What are you most proud of this week?

Are you on track for conquering the big picture milestones you set for this sprint? Could you have done anything differently?

Did you stay on top of your health and maintain your new habit?

Did you have any big insights or serendipitous moments?

FOR NEXT WEEK:

☐
☐
☐
☐
☐
☐
☐
☐
☐
☐
☐
☐
☐
☐

I am...

Success breeds confidence.

– BERYL MARKHAM, AVIATOR

MONDAY	TUESDAY	WEDNESDAY
TODAY'S TOP 5:	TODAY'S TOP 5:	TODAY'S TOP 5:
☐	☐	☐
☐	☐	☐
☐	☐	☐
☐	☐	☐
☐	☐	☐
DWELL IN GRATITUDE:	DWELL IN GRATITUDE:	DWELL IN GRATITUDE:
♡	♡	♡
♡	♡	♡
♡	♡	♡

MASTERY & WELL-BEING:	MASTERY & WELL-BEING:	MASTERY & WELL-BEING:
H2O ⎍ ⎍ ⎍ ⎍ ⎍ ⎍ ⎍ ⎍	H2O ⎍ ⎍ ⎍ ⎍ ⎍ ⎍ ⎍ ⎍	H2O ⎍ ⎍ ⎍ ⎍ ⎍ ⎍ ⎍ ⎍
EXERCISE 🏃 🏃 🏃 🏃 🏃 🏃	EXERCISE 🏃 🏃 🏃 🏃 🏃 🏃	EXERCISE 🏃 🏃 🏃 🏃 🏃 🏃
15 15 15 15 15 15	15 15 15 15 15 15	15 15 15 15 15 15
☐ DAILY HABIT	☐ DAILY HABIT	☐ DAILY HABIT

DELIVERABLES:

RECEIVABLES:

BIG PICTURE PRIORITIES TO FOCUS ON:			SPRINT WEEK 10/12

DATE

THURSDAY	FRIDAY	SATURDAY

THURSDAY

TODAY'S TOP 5:
- ☐
- ☐
- ☐
- ☐
- ☐

DWELL IN GRATITUDE:
- ♡
- ♡
- ♡

MASTERY & WELL-BEING:

H2O ☐☐☐☐☐☐☐☐

EXERCISE 🏃🏃🏃🏃🏃🏃
15 15 15 15 15 15

☐ DAILY HABIT

FRIDAY

TODAY'S TOP 5:
- ☐
- ☐
- ☐
- ☐
- ☐

DWELL IN GRATITUDE:
- ♡
- ♡
- ♡

MASTERY & WELL-BEING:

H2O ☐☐☐☐☐☐☐☐

EXERCISE 🏃🏃🏃🏃🏃🏃
15 15 15 15 15 15

☐ DAILY HABIT

SATURDAY

SUNDAY

WEEKLY REFLECTION:

How are you feeling about the progress made towards your big picture milestones this week?

😁 😍 😊 😐 😟 😢

What are you most proud of this week?

Are you on track for conquering the big picture milestones you set for this sprint? Could you have done anything differently?

Did you stay on top of your health and maintain your new habit?

Did you have any big insights or serendipitous moments?

FOR NEXT WEEK:
- ☐
- ☐
- ☐
- ☐
- ☐
- ☐
- ☐
- ☐
- ☐
- ☐
- ☐
- ☐
- ☐
- ☐

I am...

The question isn't who's going to let me; it's who is going to stop me.

– AYN RAND, AUTHOR

MONDAY	TUESDAY	WEDNESDAY
TODAY'S TOP 5:	TODAY'S TOP 5:	TODAY'S TOP 5:
☐	☐	☐
☐	☐	☐
☐	☐	☐
☐	☐	☐
☐	☐	☐
DWELL IN GRATITUDE:	DWELL IN GRATITUDE:	DWELL IN GRATITUDE:
♡	♡	♡
♡	♡	♡
♡	♡	♡

MASTERY & WELL-BEING:	MASTERY & WELL-BEING:	MASTERY & WELL-BEING:
H2O ⊔⊔⊔⊔⊔⊔⊔	H2O ⊔⊔⊔⊔⊔⊔⊔	H2O ⊔⊔⊔⊔⊔⊔⊔
EXERCISE 15 15 15 15 15 15 15	EXERCISE 15 15 15 15 15 15 15	EXERCISE 15 15 15 15 15 15 15
☐ DAILY HABIT	☐ DAILY HABIT	☐ DAILY HABIT

DELIVERABLES:

RECEIVABLES:

BIG PICTURE PRIORITIES TO FOCUS ON:

DATE

THURSDAY

TODAY'S TOP 5:
- [ ]
- [ ]
- [ ]
- [ ]
- [ ]

DWELL IN GRATITUDE:
- ♡
- ♡
- ♡

MASTERY & WELL-BEING:

H2O ▭ ▭ ▭ ▭ ▭ ▭ ▭ ▭

EXERCISE 15 15 15 15 15 15 15

- [ ] DAILY HABIT

FRIDAY

TODAY'S TOP 5:
- [ ]
- [ ]
- [ ]
- [ ]
- [ ]

DWELL IN GRATITUDE:
- ♡
- ♡
- ♡

MASTERY & WELL-BEING:

H2O ▭ ▭ ▭ ▭ ▭ ▭ ▭ ▭

EXERCISE 15 15 15 15 15 15 15

- [ ] DAILY HABIT

SATURDAY

SUNDAY

WEEKLY REFLECTION:

How are you feeling about the progress made towards your big picture milestones this week?

What are you most proud of this week?

Are you on track for conquering the big picture milestones you set for this sprint? Could you have done anything differently?

Did you stay on top of your health and maintain your new habit?

Did you have any big insights or serendipitous moments?

FOR NEXT WEEK:
- [ ]
- [ ]
- [ ]
- [ ]
- [ ]
- [ ]
- [ ]
- [ ]
- [ ]
- [ ]
- [ ]
- [ ]
- [ ]
- [ ]

I am...

Courage is like a muscle.
We strengthen it by use.

– RUTH GORDON, ACTRESS AND PLAYWRIGHT

MONDAY	TUESDAY	WEDNESDAY

TODAY'S TOP 5:

☐
☐
☐
☐
☐

DWELL IN GRATITUDE:

♡
♡
♡

TODAY'S TOP 5:

☐
☐
☐
☐
☐

DWELL IN GRATITUDE:

♡
♡
♡

TODAY'S TOP 5:

☐
☐
☐
☐
☐

DWELL IN GRATITUDE:

♡
♡
♡

MASTERY & WELL-BEING:

H2O ☐ ☐ ☐ ☐ ☐ ☐

EXERCISE 🏃 🏃 🏃 🏃 🏃 🏃
          15 15 15 15 15 15

☐ DAILY HABIT

MASTERY & WELL-BEING:

H2O ☐ ☐ ☐ ☐ ☐ ☐

EXERCISE 🏃 🏃 🏃 🏃 🏃 🏃
          15 15 15 15 15 15

☐ DAILY HABIT

MASTERY & WELL-BEING:

H2O ☐ ☐ ☐ ☐ ☐ ☐

EXERCISE 🏃 🏃 🏃 🏃 🏃 🏃
          15 15 15 15 15 15

☐ DAILY HABIT

DELIVERABLES:

RECEIVABLES:

BIG PICTURE PRIORITIES TO FOCUS ON:	SPRINT WEEK 12/12

DATE

THURSDAY

TODAY'S TOP 5:

☐
☐
☐
☐
☐

DWELL IN GRATITUDE:

♡
♡
♡

MASTERY & WELL-BEING:

H2O ⊔ ⊔ ⊔ ⊔ ⊔ ⊔ ⊔

EXERCISE 🏃 🏃 🏃 🏃 🏃 🏃 🏃
       15 15 15 15 15 15 15

☐ DAILY HABIT

FRIDAY

TODAY'S TOP 5:

☐
☐
☐
☐
☐

DWELL IN GRATITUDE:

♡
♡
♡

MASTERY & WELL-BEING:

H2O ⊔ ⊔ ⊔ ⊔ ⊔ ⊔ ⊔

EXERCISE 🏃 🏃 🏃 🏃 🏃 🏃 🏃
       15 15 15 15 15 15 15

☐ DAILY HABIT

SATURDAY

SUNDAY

WEEKLY REFLECTION:

How are you feeling about the progress made towards your big picture milestones this week?

What are you most proud of this week?

Are you on track for conquering the big picture milestones you set for this sprint? Could you have done anything differently?

Did you stay on top of your health and maintain your new habit?

Did you have any big insights or serendipitous moments?

FOR NEXT WEEK:

☐
☐
☐
☐
☐
☐
☐
☐
☐
☐
☐
☐
☐
☐

That's another year conquered. You did it!

What are you most proud of achieving this past year?

What would you say is the most valuable thing you learned this year?

What are you most grateful for right now?

What didn't quite go according to plan that you're ready to let go of now?

What Big Picture Goals did you complete, and how does your life look and feel now that you accomplished those goals?

What are your top five best memories of the last year?

What new habits did you form that have made a big difference in your life and business?

What are you most excited about for a fresh, new year ahead?

CONCLUSION

What is it about endings that feel so bittersweet, Conqueror?

When we finish good books, it feels like saying good-bye to an old friend.

When we finish big projects, it can feel as if we'd given wings to something that takes on a life of its own. And when we finish planners, we just can't believe how far we've come.

I want to make sure you take some time to congratulate yourself and celebrate. You *did* it. All of it. The deep work, the goal and milestone setting, the heart-focused action sprints. *Congratulations!*

AND, ON BEHALF OF THE ENTIRE WORLD WHO GETS TO WITNESS YOUR BRILLIANCE, THANK YOU.

Thank you for believing in yourself enough to make this happen.

Thank you for showing up and putting your work out there.

Thank you for committing to action, to yourself, and to the big dreams that have been kindled in your heart and in your head for far too long.

Completing your sprints and making amazing things happen, several times over, is a huge accomplishment. Don't forget that.

Now . . . what happens next?

First off, I recommend you do a very special something to reward yourself for everything you've achieved! Take yourself on a little vacation, to a nice dinner, or to an event or conference you've been itching to attend.

Then, I suggest you go back over everything you've made happen in the past year. Acknowledge it. Let it sink in. This will help you remember how far you've come—and just how far you can still go.

And, last but not least . . . pick up a clean and fresh *Conquer Your Year* planner for your next fifty-two weeks of conquering goals, creating powerful habits, improving your health and well-being, and so much more.

It would be my honor to help you move your work and life into even *higher* levels of possibility, love, and passion-focused profit.

Take time to rest. You can start again tomorrow, next week, or next month. But whatever you do—don't stop moving.

You know the world needs you more than ever, and I know your best is yet to come.

With gratitude,

Natalie

IMAGE AND DESIGN CREDITS

This page should be considered an extension of the copyright page.

Interior design by Amanda Genther. Assistant designer Jessica Suhr.

Water icon:

https://creativemarket.com/miumiu/64522-Hand-drawn-water-icons

Fitness icon:

https://creativemarket.com/miumiu/64525-Hand-drawn-fitness-icons

Emoticons:

https://creativemarket.com/Ctrlx/321432-Emoticons-monochrome

ABOUT THE AUTHOR

Natalie MacNeil is an Emmy Award-winning media entrepreneur and the creator of SheTakesOnTheWorld.com. She Takes on the World was recognized by Forbes.com on "Top 100 Websites for Entrepreneurs" and was also honored with "Website of the Year" at the Stevie Awards for Women in Business. Natalie is frequently quoted and interviewed in the media. She has appeared in top media outlets like *Elle* magazine, *Glamour*, *Time, Inc.*, *Forbes*, *The Wall Street Journal*, CNN, and *Entrepreneur*, to name a few. She is also the author of *The Conquer Kit* (TarcherPerigee) and *She Takes on the World*.

© Hilary Gauld Commercial

Connect with Natalie:

Facebook.com/nataliemacneil

Twitter @nataliemacneil

Periscope @nataliemacneil

YouTube.com/shetakesontheworld

Instagram @nataliemacneil

Snapchat @nataliemacneil